Sacred Smoke

Sacred Smoke

Clear Away Negative Energies and Purify
Body, Mind, and Spirit

AMY BLACKTHORN

WEISER
BOOKS

This edition first published in 2019 by Weiser Books, an imprint of
Red Wheel/Weiser, LLC
With offices at:
65 Parker Street, Suite 7
Newburyport, MA 01950
www.redwheelweiser.com

ISBN: 978-1-57863-680-8

Library of Congress Cataloging-in-Publication Data available upon request.

Cover and interior design by Kathryn Sky-Peck
Cover image using photo by Serena Williamson /Alamy Stock Photo
Typeset in Centaur

Printed in Canada
MAR
10 9 8 7 6 5 4 3 2 1

To the Adventures of Friends,
the Friends I Have Adventures with,
and the Grand Adventure that Is Life.

A day without fragrance is a day lost.

—Ancient Egyptian saying

CONTENTS

Acknowledgments

I give my warmest thanks to the following:

To my team at Weiser, who take my harebrained schemes and help me develop them into fully formed works of art. To Judika, a dear friend and an incredible editor, who takes my calls at two in the morning. To Sam M, adventurer and friend, forever in pursuit of those book stands. To Josh and Kane, the best cheerleaders and friends anyone could ask for, I love you. To Kristin, thank you for being my 3 a.m. sounding board, my perfume coconspirator, and my dearest friend. To TAM and Whitemarsh Theod for being unwavering bastions of support and love for all these years. To Lori P and the MVers as well as Jesse B at Finding Avalon for embracing my teaching methods and heart. To my own little family, especially Leeloo keeping me company while I wrote this. To the readers who asked for this, thank you.

Introduction

So, why incense? Why bathe in the smoke of these fragrant plants, resins, and flowers? Sacred smoke is a tool of magic and of transformation.

Throughout time people have embraced their sense of smell in new and exciting ways, using delicate flowers, plants, and resins to uplift them and open their eyes to the world and the universe. The plants they grew were offered as a dedication, a sacrifice to the gods to have their prayers heard. The ancient Egyptians burned three different incenses morning, noon, and night: frankincense, myrrh, and kyphi. We can see this idea carrying over in more recent times in many indigenous cultures, the Catholic Church, Pagan religions, and New Age practices. And as we've learned more about plants, their practical benefits have also played a part. During World War II, nurses in makeshift hospitals burned bundles of lavender stems to get rid of "bad air," as they knew lavender was antiseptic and hoped burning the dried plant would attain the same results. To some extent it did.

No matter your faith, practicing with sacred smoke is a powerful way to make your intentions known and support change in your life. Incense isn't just an alternative to air freshener. Sacred smoke is a shared journey between yourself, the plants around you, and, if you choose, your god or gods—it creates an opportunity to experience and listen to the natural rhythm of the earth beneath our feet. This book seeks to connect you with these things.

An argument between friends can be hashed out over calming lavender smoke. A home can find prosperity in the embrace of burning clove powder. Space can be consecrated with the grace and devotional power of cedar. Every ritual or occasion can be tailored to the language of scent.

Sacred smoke isn't required for intention work, rituals, and spells, but it certainly does lend an air of the sacred to separate us from our day-to-day, doesn't it? We need the trappings of good ritual sometimes. It gives a flair for the dramatic in a way that turns off the laundry lists, the "honey dos," and the running commentary. And it does all of this in a way that all the social media photo filters in the world couldn't accomplish—by opening up the sense that draws most powerfully on our memory and associations. Remember, the magic is in us, not in the candles, cauldrons, wands, or incense.

Magic is a word you'll see a lot here. Magic is causing change in accordance with your will. Magic is the ability to take control of what is happening in your life, shuffle those cards, and deal again to ask for a new hand, from God, the Goddess, the universe—whomever.

Burning incense can offer us a retreat-like atmosphere or it can tell us we are that extra in *The Craft* as we have always secretly imagined. It can distract the five-year-old that lives in the back of all of our brains, yelling for stickers, candy, a movie, or something to color while we do the Work. It gives us permission to let everything else take a back seat, even for a few moments. Most important, it can flip that switch in our brain that quiets the rest of the day and reminds us that now is our time.

What we're doing here isn't just burning plants. We are forming a connection to the earth under our feet. We are connecting to the people around us, in our homes, and in our lives. We are using these plants to remind us that we are alive and that we have agency. We can demand better in our lives, and we require better.

You just need time (not a lot, I promise), energy (just barely more than it takes to get off the couch from your latest streaming binge), and the materials. It's getting the information to know what to do that is the vital part—and that's right here in what you're holding, so you're already halfway there.

When we start to delve into the herbal correspondences, the critical part is to not let it get overwhelming. Take it in small pieces. Remember, the goal is not to try to memorize everything. The goal is to work with the plant materials that you enjoy and get to know three or so elements inside and out before moving on to another three. That way you know those herbs or resins and can really start to put them together in new and exciting ways.

This simple way of approaching those plants that make you happy and make your heart sing is much more viable and nourishing than expecting anyone to memorize any books on incense or herbs. That's setting you up for failure, and I'll never do that. Cross my heart.

Just remember to stop and think about your ultimate goal. Write it down if you can before starting any work so you can really make sure you've thought about it from all the angles. We don't have the luxury of blaming anyone or anything but ourselves for our actions. There is no "the devil made me do it" here. It's all about personal responsibility.

How are you going to get your burn on and start on all this life-changing? You can do these activities any day, anytime. I'd say anywhere, but I'm pretty sure the health department frowns on you lighting up your favorite herbal bundle to cleanse all the other restaurant patrons of any lingering negativity. But outside of commonsense no-no's, there really aren't a lot of rules about where to use cleansing, sacred smoke. Any area of your home can serve as a retreat space that can be enhanced by herbal smoke. Sacred smoke in a bedroom a half-hour before bed allows the room to be fragranced, but the place isn't so smoky that it makes it hard to feel safe falling asleep. (As long as we're following the rules about fire safety, everything should be okay.) In the kitchen, incense can remind us of the sacred tasks of nourishing our body, mind, and spirit, while clearing out lingering odors of strongly scented dishes. When the living room is graced with a delicate scent of dried herbs, it gives us permission to relax and let go of the stresses of the day with a good book or a television show before retiring for the night.

Tracking lunar phases isn't necessary when doing intention work with herbal smoke, but that can help if you work with them already. It's the choice of incense components that is essential, as what you pick speaks to the intent behind each change. For example, lavender and frankincense can be ground together in a mortar and pestle and then burned to protect secrets, promote balance, or even stimulate the scales of justice. In these pages you'll learn about these and many other options. You'll also learn that just because something smells good, doesn't mean it will be great to burn. Dried peppermint smells good in sachets, but without accompanying herbs in your blend, the heat of the smoke and the cold of the menthol can create a confusing smell in your nose. Not everything will smell the same burning as it does dried.

Inside this book you'll find the following:

Brass Tacks. These sections offer helpful and practical ways to practice the techniques that are foundational not only to developing this sacred smoke practice, but also to the focus for the specific chapter in which you find yourself.

Changing Seasons: Rites for the Passage of Time. These rites are provided for working through the seasons and evolving practice over time.

Well-Being: Checking on Energetic Health. Learn techniques to check in on the energetic health of yourself, your home, and your hearth so negative energies don't have time to build up. With regular attention and cleansings, things don't have the time to get to problematic levels.

Featured Herbs and Resins. Each chapter shares a featured herb and resin or wood aligning with its theme so that we can delve a little deeper into the relationship with those plant allies and learn more about them one-on-one.

MORE ABOUT MAGIC

Story time! When I was about sixteen, I came "out of the broom closet" to my family and started talking about magic. When it came time to talk one-on-one with my fifteen-year-old sister, she was very pragmatic about the whole thing. "Let's see it, then," she said, arms crossed and stern look on her face. It wasn't that she didn't believe me; she wanted to understand but just needed context.

"Okay, what if we were in a drought and needed a bit of rain and a bit of wind to help the ecosystem? That would be good, right?" I asked.

"Sure, I suppose."

"Well, magic and spells are enacted prayers, so I could ask for rain to help ease the burden of the drought. In this case, it would be appealing to the gods rather than attempting to influence because of the delicate balance of nature." I make that wishy-washy gesture that only teens can really master.

"So how would you know if your spell worked?" she challenged.

"When it rained," I replied.

"No, how would you know that *you* made it happen?" she countered. I get the direct stare that says the Sagittarius brain is now engaged.

"Magic isn't about credit, gold stars, or a chore chart. What I had asked for happened. I give thanks and move on. I may choose to record it in my journal if it felt particularly noteworthy, but I know what I needed came to be, and that's that."

When it comes to measuring the results of our intention, the only yardstick that matters is our own. No one else's opinion, measurements, or results can compare or reflect against your own. It's not necessarily a matter of experience, though years of it will help you avoid the more common pitfalls of practice.

Accessible Purification

What Everyone Needs to Know Before
Starting a Cleansing Practice

Your sense of smell is the particular sense that connects you both to your past and to those around you. Our sense of smell connects to our oldest understanding of the world around us, and it is the most important one we have. We used that sense of smell as infants to connect to our mothers before we could even see, to tie emotions to places, and more. Home has a scent. Mothers and fathers have a scent. Partners have a fragrance all their own. Every day we use fragrant connections to further those bonds. Using the rituals of daily life, we strengthen our relationship with that scent concerning each person.

Recently my friend Sue was clearing out her supplies and asked if I could use a box of essential oils, knowing I was working on *Blackthorn's Botanical Magic* at the time, and I readily agreed. Once I arrived home, I grabbed the first bottle in the box without looking at the label, pulled off the lid, and smelled. Unbidden the corners of my mouth curled up into a giant grin, and my eyes twinkled with past memories. That particular container I had chosen was bottled summer walks to the library with my mom and three sisters for movies or books, and on the way home we'd stop at the neighborhood treat—a snowball. In a small outbuilding on the side of the street, crushed ice was covered in flavored syrups and occasionally marshmallow fluff. This barn-painted building sported forty-seven flavors, but for me and my mom there was always only one choice: egg custard. This bottle of benzoin oil I had just smelled was no mere essential oil, but a time machine. Such is the power of our sense of smell.

We are all creatures of art, poetry, and emotion, and I can prove it to you. Grab your favorite journal or the nearest pad of paper, and keep them close by while you close your eyes and inhale deeply through your nose. Imagine your favorite smells. We all have them. Pick your top five. It works best with your eyes closed to block out distractions. Go ahead and make a list with a little bit of space for your thoughts between each. Once you have your five favorite smells, I want you to concentrate on each one. I'll bet that rather than a smell, what rises in your mind is a memory. Even smells that aren't associated with traditional perfumes or essential oils have their place in this exercise. Musty basements can be family game nights, fertile fields can be the joy of playing outside with our best childhood friends. This journal entry isn't about judging flowers or perfumes, it's about connecting scent and memory. Every thought is the right one. Do you smell water? Is it the tangy metal of a summer sprinkler cooling the air around you or the local stream kids waded into to cool off? Floral doesn't always mean sweet; it could be the sharp minty spice of lavender. Pull out each memory and touch, taste, and experience it to the fullest.

Now that you're all fired up with the scents you love, it may seem like the most natural thing to go grab some dried, formerly green stuff, light it on fire, wave it around, and call it a day. However, before you run out and start ripping the weeds out of the sidewalk or stalking the local shop looking for any of "those stick things," there are a few more basics you'll need to know.

Terms of the Trade

If you've picked up anything about using sacred smoke before opening this book, you may have heard it called *smudging*. Indigenous people and First Nations peoples have an indigenous practice called smudging that is sacred to them. If you are not a member of an indigenous tribe and/or trained in that practice, it won't be smudging: it is smoke cleansing, smoke bathing, smoke rituals—you get the idea. We're here to learn how to build our own practice without appropriating another culture's. With the indigenous women I've spoken to about this project, the lessons have been many. Every culture has its own practices for sacred smoke, and they deserve their own time and attention. There is room for respect and growth without appropriation. For this book, we will talk about smoke practice in other ways with different terms.

Another practice has gotten more attention in recent years, especially with much-needed conversations about appropriate ritual observances and cultural identity, and this is *Saining*. Saining is a Scottish folk magic practice, which on the surface can have a similar outward appearance to smoke cleansing; however, the two are not the same thing. Saining uses the elements of nature to carry out blessings and charms. Though the word *Sain* sounds like "sin," it does not mean removal of evil, but connotes bestowing of the good or beneficial. *Sain* comes from the Scots-Gaelic term meaning "to charm." While Saining uses smoke bundles and other sacred smoke practices—as in the idea of driving pasture animals between two bonfires at spring and fall (Beltane and Samhain) to purify them for the next six months—that is not the only method it employs. Seawater and other blessed waters, candles, wood from pine trees, and other sources of charming are also used. Saining is a beautiful traditional folk practice in its own right, and most importantly not a loan word to replace *smudging*.

The materials for smoke cleansing come in different forms. Let's look at those and what they each mean.

Sticks. This is a general term referencing a stick of traditional incense where a sliver of bamboo is rolled in pine sawdust and scented so that consumers can burn it in their homes to create scented smoke.

Incense. This is a scented amalgamation of materials burned to produce a pleasing odor, with or without ritual intent.

Smoke bundles. Stick-like tools that can be made out of one or more plant materials and burned so that the smoke can bring about a desired change in the environment. They are usually 8–12 inches in length and 1–2 inches in diameter and bound with string and can be made at home or purchased. (More on that later!) Simply touch a lit match or lighter to the far end for a moment or two to get the bundle lit, and then blow it out until it starts to smoke. (This may need to be repeated, as these herbs don't have a heat source to keep them burning and are loosely packed, so that the flame may not be sustained.)

Resins. The dried sap of several species of trees is commonly found in teardrop shapes and is a usual ingredient in incense. Remember when burning these tears, less is more. Start with one tear and add more as needed. Their smoke will be much thicker than traditional incense sticks.

A Note on Ethical Consumption

It's important to consider where the plants you will be burning come from. Poaching of threatened species, overharvesting, and trespass on native lands are all too common. Get the facts on the plants you plan to use. Be sure you are not supporting harmful farming practices. Labels that say "wildcrafted" can be misleading, so double-check that this is not just window dressing for unethical practices.

There are many ways to be sure the plant you want to use can be employed with little to no negative impact on the floriculture or ecosystem where it is found.

1. **Grow it yourself.** We'll go into this more in chapter 7, but plants like white sage are easy to get going and sometimes available from garden centers. White sage grows in the desert, so don't worry if you don't have a green thumb. You have options.

2. **Buy from an ethical supplier.** There are indigenous/tribal suppliers of things like white sage that are supporting their communities through their sales. Meanwhile, I have found white sage bundles for a few dollars in the same mall stores as frat party supplies like beer bongs, flip-flops, shot glasses, and "adult novelties." I am sure they take as much time making sure their white sage isn't poached as they do that their bikinis aren't made in sweatshops—which is to say, none. Walk into your local New Age shop and ask them where they source their herb bundles. Ask how they know they are ethically sourced. If you use a small business online retailer, email them. I'm sure they'll be just as happy to talk to you. Big-box stores often don't have that kind of information about sourcing on the ground floor.

How Does Smoke Purify?

There are a few different ways.

1. **Physically purifying.** Heat from the burning materials is very physically purifying, and the process releases volatile oils from the plant materials that have antibacterial and antimicrobial properties as well.

2. **Energetically purifying.** Each plant material used in incense, smoke, or cleansing is going to have a different energetic association. Some are associated with the elements of earth, air, fire, or water; other are associated with protection, money, grounding, and other intentions. So there are a few uses for burning these materials other than merely purification. Pick the material to match your intention.

3. **Emotionally purifying.** Our sense of smell ties in directly to the limbic system, the part of the brain where all of our emotions come from. Why is that? When we smell something, we are unpacking all of our memories, looking for the last time we remember smelling it. Our sense of smell is really a trip down memory lane. That's why sense memories are such strong stimuli. Our sense of smell is 90 percent emotion and 10 percent recall.

Tools of the Trade

Let's go shopping!

Fire-resistant is the key word here. We will be working with fire, and even though we will never leave burning materials unattended, embers can and do happen.

This is what you'll need:

Incense charcoal. It will come in rolls and usually looks like it has been wrapped in foil. And don't buy the pretty abalone shell to put it in—that is a tool for the indigenous cultures of (mainly)

the Pacific Northwest and has branched out to include other native and First Nations groups, along with feathers and smudge fans that are collected in ways that are sacred to each group. It is not appropriate. It also does not work for what I am discussing as the charcoal gets too hot for an organic container, and it will be destroyed.

Make sure to use tongs to light the charcoal—seriously. The charcoal contains something called saltpeter (potassium nitrate) to make sure it ignites quickly and burns evenly. So you will need to hold it over a fire source for a few seconds to a minute, depending on your charcoal. Also once the package of charcoal has been opened, remember to keep it in a small sealed container such as a resealable bag to keep moisture out, or else the saltpeter will absorb ambient humidity and the charcoal will no longer ignite.

A brazier (not to be confused with a brassiere). This is a container for hot coals, commonly made from brass or pottery, and the best ones have a brass screen for the charcoal to sit on so that the incense charcoal gets oxygen to all sides and continues to burn evenly. Keep in mind that even though they are made to contain hot coals, they're going to get really hot too. The ones designed for use by churches will have chains to hang them up with, but if you are planning to set yours on a counter or tabletop, make sure it has a heatproof material to sit on such as a tile.

Ornamental tongs. For incense charcoal these will often be sold with a similarly sized spoon used for scooping incense resin. Trust me, you don't want to sacrifice one of Aunt Suzy's good silver to be covered with sticky resin: it'll never be the same.

Windproof lighter. These lighters are different from traditional lighters. They sound like a small jet engine taking off and will have your materials, whether those are charcoal or herbs, lit evenly and quickly.

Mortar and pestle. This pair of stone tools is used to grind together herbs and resins to get a uniform size and texture. They are usually constructed of marble, granite, or another hard stone. It is possible to find them in hardwoods too, but resist the temptation. The tough resins in these rites, rituals, and recipes are not only pointed and can damage the wood, but if you decide to add oil of any kind, it can seep into the wood and taint any subsequent blends.

Bottles, jars, and labels. Once you start blending your own cleansing smokes and incenses, you'll need to bottle them and label them so that you know not only what you intended them to do, but also whether they worked.

Notebook and pens. And speaking of working, once you start your practice, writing down your recipes as well as how well they worked is going to be an essential part of the process. If you have a formula that works incredibly well, but the recipe is lost to the ages, that's a heck of a shame.

    Sacred Smoke

Featured Herb: Lavender

Lavandula angustifolia.

France, England, United States. Associated with Venus.

Lavender is known as a calming herb with antiseptic properties, as well as something your local yoga studios use in essential oil for balance, centering, and peace. But this plant is also burned for divination, clairvoyance, psychic development, and strength. It reveals the secrets of the universe. It has a similar action on the brain as hops, which you'll probably remember is also in beer—so a little bit is a stimulant and a lot will knock you out for the count. As with most flowers, it's associated with love, but without the strong scent that many flowers carry. It has a low moisture content, so it is much easier to dry for burning without the molding risk of roses. Be careful with lavender, however, because the buds are small cylinders and prone to pop when exposed to heat. So if you are making herb bundles for smoke purposes, use the leaves and stems only. Strip the flowers for use on charcoal and still monitor these carefully or you will wind up with herbal sparklers and potentially small burns on carpets or rugs when they spit fiery bits.

Featured Resin: Amber

Pinus succinifera. India.

Associated with water, love, happiness, and soul mates.

Amber resonates with attraction—even drawing customers to your business—and emotional strength and is useful for past-life journeying, friendship, and inner strength. In times of emotional turmoil, reach deep for memories of happiness and times when you felt loved before lighting some amber incense. It can be challenging to find true amber incense rather than scented sawdust incense. I suggest something along the lines of Fred Soll®'s Resin on a Stick®. If you are looking for psychic protection, amber is also the one to reach for. If the resin is hard to come by, diffusing the essential oil in an aromatherapy diffuser will do the same thing, but won't have the same waft (distance the scent is carried), so consider turning off the diffuser and moving it hourly. Make sure to search for the essential oil by the Latin name to help weed out fragrance oil sellers. Also look for dark glass bottles and lot numbers. Dark glass is used to block ultraviolet light that will cause oils to spoil faster. Fragrance oils come in clear glass containers that list the brand name and do not list lot numbers for quality control.

Smoke
Bathing
Starting with the Self before
Reaching Outward

A s with everything, we'll start with strengthening the self. Ready Freddy? 'Cause this is about to get bumpy.

I know, you saw some gorgeous blonde in a video from Coachella waving a smoking herb bundle and thought this self-fulfillment stuff was going to be easy, right? Well, it isn't. So buckle up. You decided you wanted to light some incense, burn some herbs, and get in touch with the Mother Goddess. Great. What happens if she picks up the phone and tells you to get your act together? Are you ready for that heart to heart? It's a toughie. If your partner isn't worshipping you like the goddess you are, or you're spending more than you're saving, or you're staying in a dead-end job because you're too scared of what you could do with your own potential, you already know what She's going to tell you: you can do better.

The kick in the pants comes when you remember it for yourself or when your tarot cards remind you of your dream of owning a bakery instead of working a soul-sucking office job. These are the times when incense and smoke bathing come into play.

That incense isn't just those crappy ten-for-a-dollar sticks you found on a gas station pit stop in a dusty highway in the middle of nowhere during that road trip with your friends that brings everyone fits of giggles when you mention it. Incense is that soul-cleansing smoke that clears out the cobwebs, the tears, and the sludge left over and leaves us waiting to be filled with creative impulses, drive, and that vital spark that animates us the way the gods intended.

Stop, drop, and roll.

Before you can do any of that soul-cleaving work, you've gotta stop what you're doing—all of it. Just stop—right where you are. Now breathe. Again. Yawn, stretch, and breathe again. We spend so much time running around, being, going, and doing that often we forget to breathe. Even when we tell each other we're making time, doing the things that we should, going to yoga, meditating, it's a competition instead of practice. We are posing for photos for social media, rather than being in the moment. My dear friend is a yogi and fond of reminding me that yoga is more than just poses. Breathe again. (This is going to be really important later . . . keep doing that mindful breath.)

But this book is about incense and energy, not yoga. You're absolutely right. I'll let you in on a secret: that's why witches talk about grounding and centering, and not meditation. Meditation is really the "it" secret to how to get better at magic. There it is, ladies and gentlemen: meditate! But no one ever wants to hear there's a simple answer, or at least they prefer an instant gratification answer and not an easy solution that takes lots of time and practice. Genuinely, grounding and centering are two different practices, and they're separate from meditation, but I'm getting ahead of myself. Breath is the foundation of effective magic.

It Begins with the Breath

This is me backing up. All life begins and ends with breath. Watch a baby breathing—their tiny belly rising and falling with each breath. They aren't thinking, "breathe in, breathe out." We breathe all day without thinking about it, but the mindful breath is so cleansing. It can help you put away the baggage of a stressful day, it can air out the laundry that has piled up in the corners of our heart—and that's before we've even gotten to the incense.

Once we've gotten comfortable with the mindful breath and remembered how uplifting it feels, we can venture forth into the realm of meditation. For the first step, I want you to grab a piece of paper, a bit of tape, and a pen and find somewhere where you won't be interrupted. Put a small dot on the paper and tape it to the wall at the height you are when you're sitting. Walk the distance of your height away from the post (no measuring tape required) and have a seat. I want you to look softly at the dot, unfocus your eyes gently, and allow the dot to become blurry. Once the dot is blurry, I want you to concentrate on your breath, and we're going to do something called *square breathing*. We're going to inhale with a four-count, hold the breath with a four-count, exhale with a four-count, and wait to inhale again with a four-count. So it's all nice and even. And do this while keeping that dot in your field of vision. Once you've practiced with a four-count, try increasing the count to five and six.

Next, try *circular breathing*. Instead of the pauses or holds in breath, simply start with slightly longer inhalation periods and exhalation periods. Inhale as you count to eight. Exhale as you count to eight. Inhale as you count to eight and repeat. If you've moved from square breathing directly into circular breathing, feel free to lie down with your eyes closed as you practice, and don't be surprised if you fall asleep. That doesn't mean you've done anything wrong. It's just the opposite, in fact: you were so relaxed that your body just did what it naturally does.

It sounds like we're doing many things all at once here, but what we're doing is allowing the brain to relax and find its own rhythm, called a *trance state*. It's very soothing and can give the person participating in the meditation the benefit of feeling like they've slept for several hours when they've meditated for a period of time. It has been shown to reduce blood pressure and more.

When the incense is burning, or smoke bundles have been lit, the columns of smoke are another visual stimulus that can induce a trancelike state. Simply slowly breathing and watching a fixed point on the other side of the smoke can produce a meditative state where it is easy for the practitioner to let go of the stressors of the day, anger, fear, and the like.

Meditating is a great way to bring yourself back to yourself. So what was that I was saying about "grounding and centering"? That's the catch-22 about cleansing practice: You want to run out and cleanse everything, right? So how do you get started? With yourself, of course. If you're mopping the floors with muddy shoes on, you're just tracking dirt everywhere and making things worse.

Grounding and Centering: Magical Tetherball

You know, it occurs to me, we say "grounding and centering," but that's backward. You have to *center* first. Centering is the gathering-up of all the disparate, excess magical energy lingering in your body, fingers, toes, and everywhere in between and focusing it in your gut, solar plexus, what have you. It's making that tiny supernova ready to go into the ground where the earth can use it.

See, this is all excess energy you aren't using. No one is suggesting sacrificing your vital life force to the planet. Nope, nuh-uh. Mom's got plenty, and she doesn't need yours. What we are saying is that if you have too much, it can cause restlessness, anxiety, jittery legs, anger, and a host of other problems, so we gather up all that excess and give it back to the Mother, who can handle it a heck of a lot better than we can. So once you've got a supernova in the center of your being, you can send it down into the earth, where it can be harmlessly absorbed back into the greater energy of the planet where it can best be used as needed.

"So, what if I'm wearing shoes, at work, in a high-rise, or on a plane?" It's all good. Seriously. It's magic. It's energy. Time, distance, and clothing choice aren't an issue. I promise. And the reverse is also true: if you feel like used dirt and could use that inner connection with the Mother, you can ground and center and reestablish that connection with Her, feel Her heartbeat, and She'll remind you She's there.

Stepping into the Fire.
(No, Not Literally.)

Once you've prepared yourself, then you know you can step forward and accept what the plant spirits are offering you. The smoke of these plants is not just scent. I want you to understand that when you are burning these leaves, resins, flowers, and oils you are consuming the essence of a plant in more than one way. Take frankincense, for example. Once the seed of a frankincense tree (*Boswellia carterii*) is planted, it takes twenty years before it starts to produce the sap that will dry into the resin that people burn as incense.

By stepping into the fire, it means that you are ready to accept what the smoke is offering you personally. By bringing it into your being as a whole, you are prepared to welcome the gifts of these plants.

So, you've collected all of the materials we outlined in chapter one. Now it's time to really jump in and get some hands-on experience. Tending the coals of your incense-burning ritual is as relevant as tending to your own needs. If you walk away from your own self-care, you'll burn out, just the same as the coals in your fire. Step away from a smoke bundle or treat it carelessly, and it can burn your house down just like an illness that goes untreated. Our spirit deserves the same respect and attention you would give a lit candle. Nurture that fire inside you, and give it some oxygen and room to grow. And anyone who makes you feel like you have to apologize for your passion? They can get the boot on the way out the door, too.

Brass Tacks: Practice Time

Grab your tools and find somewhere you can be alone for a few minutes. You'll need your notebook, pen, tongs, incense charcoal, windproof lighter (if possible), some lavender and/or powdered clove, and your fireproof container. Grab one charcoal disc *with the tongs* (trust me on this: the saltpeter in the charcoal means that the spark is going to travel *fast* and you don't want to be holding it when it does).

Light the disc. Now's the time when you realize why I specified the windproof lighter: A regular lighter means you're going

---

THE IMPORTANCE OF FIRE SAFETY

Everyone wants to jump into the part where the exciting things happen, lighting things on fire, making the magic happen. Before we can do that there have to be ground rules, fire safety, and other helpful things. If you're going to burn an herb bundle, make sure you have something to catch the ashes. It doesn't have to be decorative or pretty; it just has to be fireproof. You can grab a plate from the Dollar Store or Goodwill, as long as it isn't flammable. You don't want to burn the rug while trying to make sure your space is as cleansed as it can to be. If you are engaging in any type of smoke practice, have a fire extinguisher handy. We are dealing with flammable material. The point is that it smolders, but when you blow on smoldering material, occasionally it will flare up, and the string that holds it together only lasts until a certain point. There comes a time when that string will give up the ghost; I'd hate for a flare-up and the string giving out to both happen at the same time, the burning material to scatter, and, well, you get the point. Safety first.

---

to be sitting here while that charcoal sputters for a few minutes. A windproof lighter creates a blue flame like a small torch and will have that puppy burning nicely in a few seconds. When you think it's burning (they can be tricky, especially if the package has been open for any length of time), blow on the charcoal and look for the telltale red glow before setting it in the fireproof container. You'll know it's still burning because you'll notice that distinct smell of ozone from the burning charcoal.

Now, grab a pinch of lavender flowers, roll them between your fingers, and notice how they release their volatile oils when just a little pressure is applied. Sprinkle them onto the burning incense charcoal for them to release those volatile oils. Lavender's associations are secrets (and their retention), balance, harmony and calm, clairvoyance, divination, and psychic development. So, the practice described earlier of breathing and watching through the smoke is really beneficial if you'd like to try and develop your intuition for a method called *scrying*. Lavender is also connected to gentleness and love because of its Venusian associations. Those volatile oils are also linked to strength and known to be stimulating to the mind. Once you let go of the things making you feel anxious or keyed up, you can give your brain the heavy lifting, so to speak.

Keep an eye on lavender flowers. I know, we always keep an eye on burning anything, especially plant material, but lavender flowers are also seeds, so they tend to pop unexpectedly and can jump out of your fireproof dish. They aren't likely to cause a fire or damage property, but we just want to be extra-careful where fire is involved.

These small pinches of light materials burn pretty fast, so you'll be able to create your own changes in the atmosphere as quickly or as slowly as you'd like. In this "get to know you" phase, think of yourself as a scent DJ trying to find the right mix for the right feelings and the perfect timing for the way you want to feel.

Time to actually bathe in the smoke. While seated, take scoops of the smoke into your hands and pour them over your head. See the tendrils of smoke curl around your hair, eyes, and ears. Scoop up more smoke, and wash it over your arms and chest, before moving on to your legs. Every time you shift to a new part of the body, see the smoke reaching the inside and outside of that body part, cleansing it and leaving it warm, whole, and safe. Repeat this for each new plant, resin, and wood as you get to know them in your sacred smoke practice.

During this time, record your thoughts and feelings in your notebook. You want to be able to refer to these notes later. If you have a negative emotion, feeling, or association surface, you want to be able to examine the nature of that experience and understand why it came to light. Remember, our sense of smell is 90 percent memory and 10 percent recognition. You're unpacking a big, dusty box of old experiences every time you take a trip down memory lane. It's helpful with painful memories to remember you aren't living that event again, you're reviewing a faded copy. You're experiencing the last time you pulled it out of the box, and you can overwrite that scent in your brain if you want to.

With the tongs, gently brush aside the now burned flower remnants. Since they're seeds, there will be flower husks left over after they have been consumed instead of ash. Grab up a pinch of ground clove and give a gentle inhale. Not too hard now, or you'll get dust up your nose and that's not fun at all. Sprinkle some of that ground clove over the charcoal and wait for the smoke to rise before closing your eyes to gently inhale its fragrance. Clove is used for dispelling negative influences, and that fiery energy is of course associated with the sun. It's excellent for hex-breaking because it burns away anything clinging to you that doesn't belong there. It's very protective because all of that fire purifies the self from anything that isn't a part of you and seals it against intrusion. Clove is also used to stimulate the mind and increase thought, mental acuity, and psychic development (so it would blend well with lavender for developing intuition!). Open your eyes and scoop a handful of the smoke over your head.

There you go: you've taken your first step toward smoke bathing. Place a bit more material on the incense burner before going further (and if you want to add the lavender and clove together, go for it). We'll need a little more smoke for practicing this part. Once you've gotten the hang of scooping that smoke over your head, wash the smoke over your arms, down your legs, and down your back.

When you are done, take a few moments to write about this experience in your notebook. As you are getting to know these practices, it is good to order your thoughts and have a way to look back at your earliest impressions. Did your feelings change during the exercise?

Changing Seasons:
Rites for the Passage of Time

So how often do you practice this smoke bathing thing that we're doing? Daily? Weekly? Monthly? As with anything that's shiny and new, you'll likely turn to it all the time once you've picked up this book and all the fabulous things that go with it. You'll be ecstatic about all the opportunities for using what you've learned and look for any excuses. Then you'll calm down and realize that there are only so many times you can thwack the smoke detector with a broom before your significant other, your dog, your cat, and the neighbors are giving you the stink eye. You calm down, come back to earth, and remember there is a time and place for everything.

A monthly cleansing ritual is more than plenty; just allow for emergency situations to arise. What's a cleansing emergency? A toxic ex could come back into town (that could be a friend or a former lover—sometimes old friends are even more traumatic than former lovers), or there could be a community tragedy or caustic protest (a specific "church" that likes to protest funerals comes to mind). Those are perfectly reasonable causes to stop, ground, and center, and reach for the incense charcoal.

"Oh, no! I'm at work when X cruddy thing happens. I can't burn incense here." It's all good, I've got you. Stop, ground, and center—just like you would before starting your ritual practice at home or with friends. Close your eyes if it's safe to do so. Excuse yourself to the restroom if you have to. If it's a more extreme case and there is anxiety involved, run the inside of your wrists under *cold* water. (Chew gum if you have it/can find it. Yes, seriously. Your sympathetic nervous system can't eat and panic at the same time. It's against the rules of people-ing. It's commonsense fight or flight: If you're "eating," then you must not be fighting for your life. Really, it'll help with the anxiety. Cross my heart. Chew slowly: no choking on the gum.) Keep running your wrists under cold water for another few moments while you breathe slowly in through your nose and out through your mouth. Think mindful breaths. Yawn if you have to (oxygen regulation!). Then start your grounding and centering just like we practiced. If you can't use incense at work and you need a touch-up, grab a partial bottle or cup of water, add a packet of salt (purifying), and dip your fingers in it. Rub some on your temples, wrists, and behind your knees if you can reach them.

Outside of emergencies, mark the change of the seasons with cleansing rites so you can move into each new quarter of the year refreshed and renewed. Just like spring cleaning, you'll have a fresh outlook and renewed vigor, having disengaged from the attachments and any lingering energetic maladies from the previous season.

Featured Herb: White Sage

Salvia apiana.

United States. Cleansing and purification of spaces and people.

Bathe in the smoke of a few dried leaves of this member of the salvia family to refresh body, mind, and spirit. White sage smells herbal and woody; it has a bite, but not as sharp as its culinary cousin.

Many ethical buyers note the "wildcrafted" labels on white sage and feel right about not supporting harmful farming practices without all the facts. White sage does not grow well in a farmed environment, so nearly all the white sage that is sold today is wild-crafted. Increasing demand is also negatively impacting the cost of the materials for the population for whom it is a sacred plant. Because of the circumstances of growth habit, climate, and potential for wildfires, this can lead to poaching, overharvesting, and trespass on native lands, just to meet demand in an ever-increasing market. It is also by no means the only salvia that can be used in this practice, and considering the pressures put on white sage from outsized demand and overharvesting, choosing one of the other options may be the most ethical choice for some.

Garden sage (*Salvia officinalis*) is less common in smoke bundles, but still a viable alternative to white sage, as is *Salvia leucantha*, or Mexican bush sage, a very soft salvia with pointed leaves extending about six to fourteen inches depending on the age and environment of the plant. This velvety member of the salvia family is much more prolific than its overharvested and contentious cousin and

Sacred Smoke

a much prettier plant to grow in your garden, with spikes of soft, vibrant purple buds that are two to three feet in length. It attracts hummingbirds and requires little care—all members of the salvia family, are drought tolerant.

Featured Resin: Myrrh

Commiphora myrrha.

Somalia. Used with frankincense since at least 1500 BCE to consecrate ritual tools, invoke meditative feelings, and purify spaces.

Myrrh is restorative, attuned to success, happiness, and good luck, and increases confidence. There is no "imposter syndrome" when the darker, more resinous scent of myrrh is around. Myrrh is used to invoke feelings of compassion and can be uplifting, so if you're down in the dumps or have had an argument with a friend and are hoping to find some middle ground, burn myrrh while you hash out what went down. It also attracts honorable behavior, so the truth will win out. Want to improve your faith in your divination? Myrrh is attuned to prophesying as well. Myrrh is also the guardian of gratitude, so feel free to burn myrrh while journaling a regular gratitude practice to cement those feelings for the long term.

Hearth and Home

Keeping Your Family Whole in Trying Times

Families can be one of the most rewarding experiences, and the most arduous. We can build each other up in unforeseen ways, but no one knows where the holes in our armor are the way family does. There is no one else we would or could serve the way we do family or things we wouldn't do without for them. Throughout this chapter we'll be talking about family, but don't let that stop you from looking at the families that we choose, as well as those of blood.

And therein lies the rub. You cannot pour from an empty cup, my dears. No matter how well-intentioned we are, no matter the lies we tell ourselves, the promises we make about taking care of our needs "later"—tomorrow, at payday, next month, or next year—that day never seems to come, does it? All for the love of family. I know how you mean it when you promise to get yourself your own needed things. "I'll get new pants later." "These shoes will last another year." What we don't realize is that in denying ourselves in the short term we are harming our families in the long term. You cannot pour from an empty cup.

Let's look at that biggest of family budget dilemmas: footwear. Kids' feet grow—pretty rapidly. Some days it seems they wake up inches taller than when they went to sleep. Things that fit when they fell asleep no longer fit when they wake up. And that includes shoes. So, for a budget-minded parent with several children—I have three sisters, I'll tell you—all needing shoes the same day, it seems that buying inexpensive shoes is the expedient way to go. You save money, the household keeps running another day. And as those young ladies grow up to be young women wearing modest footwear, they learn inexpensive footwear doesn't last long, and when it wears out, it gets replaced.

Instead let's look at that from a standpoint of the now single, adult woman who has to provide only for herself. Instead of buying one discount pair of shoes every few months, she buys one quality pair of shoes that will last years and has now saved money by spending a little more upfront.

What does this have to do with your smoke and plant allies? Look at the materials that are available in the shops around you. There are stores that only sell stick incense (and there are some amazing brands out there, you just have to experiment until you find them), but with a little outlay of money upfront you can get some quality material that will last a good long time and not only save money, but provide a fulfilling practice and a connection to the world around you. Once you have a burner and some charcoal, you can restock your resins for the same cost as keeping up with your stick incense habit without leaving a forest of those bamboo sticks behind.

Making Your Own Sticks

Another way to be smart with your budget and get to know the process on your own is to make your own sticks. However, please do more research than watching one video online before deciding that your first experiment in smoke cleansing should be with something homemade.

Things to consider before making your own:

1. **Bulky materials.** When you work with things like whole roses, they can mold in the middle of a stick really easily. When a rose petal burns, it doesn't smell like a rose garden. If you are really keen to work with rose energy, a rose petal or two in the middle of the stick will be better than trying to get a bud to burn.

2. **Things that go pop.** Lavender smells nice when it burns over charcoal. However, don't put lavender flowers on the stems in your sticks. The flowers pop when they heat up and can burn you or jump out of the stick and burn rugs, floors, countertops, or other surfaces. Instead, strip the flowers from the stem and burn the flowers over charcoal. The cleaned stems and

leaves can then go into the cleansing smoke bundle, where they can still lend that beautiful lavender scent. Some companies already sell bundles of lavender stems to purify and calm.

3. **Doing your homework.** Before trying any new project, research. Half the fun of learning a new skill is allowing yourself to revel in being new at it. Anytime you want to include something in your smoke practice or add it to your homemade sticks, try it out with the charcoal first to make sure the scent of the burning material is the same as you thought it would be.

4. **Function over form.** Most of the how-to videos you'll find are more concerned with making something that looks pretty, rather than a bundle that functions as needed. Pretty does not equal smelling the best when burning. They show a picturesque location where a happy host brings a well-curated pile of plant material to the camera and constructs a monstrosity that will never dry, will entirely mold, and, though gorgeous now, will smell awful if burned.

5. **Forming the stick.** It isn't necessary to choose a backbone plant with a woody stem to hold your bundle together; once it has dried, it will hold its shape. Try rosemary and mint, rosemary and lavender, or lavender and lemon balm for your first combinations. Start layering your plant material until you have a solid foundation, roughly two fingers wide by a hand length tall. Remember, this will shrink as it dries, but

a stick that is too thick won't dry properly and may mold. Also be sure to tie the end at the bottom because once it starts burning, it is going to want to unravel. Wind a spiral one finger width wide up one side and back down the other with a natural cotton twine or string. By the time you make it back down to where you started, you can tie it off to the original knot. See the section on drying for the refrigeration technique for a foolproof way to dry any sticks you make.

The incense recipes in chapter 8 offer a number of combinations for you to try.

Handy Household Helpers

How many women are wearing diamonds? It's not as many as it used to be, but it is still the traditional ring of engagement, weddings, and even anniversary. How handy it is that the symbol of stewardship over a household is magically useful too! Diamonds are attuned to courage, fair judgment, averting discord, overcoming pestilence—does any of this sound familiar? Women aren't just magical, they are aided in battle.

When stones are run under cold water (such as when we're washing our hands), it cleanses them of negativity and grounds the wearer for the next round of battle. Diamonds help the bearer see through enchantment—so slimy door-to-door salesmen have no chance, nor do spam emails. Diamonds help to repel ghosts, dispel illusions, calm panic, and expel sorrow. They can also help give your third eye—the theoretical seat of psychic ability—a boost as they have a connection to clairaudience (clear hearing) and clairvoyance (clear seeing) as well as altered states of consciousness.

If you want to encourage any of these traits in your stone, simply hold it in your dominant hand while centering the little bits of the scattered energy in your body (refer back to chapter 2). Picture the need you have as simply as you can—"just judge" or "calm down," for example—and send the energy you focused into the stone.

There's a beautiful herb that is found in both medicinal and magical circles that has a long history with both hearth and family: *Vitex agnus-castus*, or chaste tree or chasteberry. This beautiful tree can grow twenty to thirty feet in height and blooms into footlong spikes of pale purple and white blossoms that are beloved by pollinators of all kinds. From butterflies and moths to hummingbirds and bees—they come from near and far to sample this spicy nectar, also called monk's pepper. This plant was grown in monastic gardens during the Middle Ages when the price of black pepper (*Piper nigrum*) was through the roof. The monks also noted that merely touching the wood, which they made into knife handles, kept them chaste, not knowing that the high estrogen content in the berries was really responsible.

Medicinally, this dried berry is used to help women with premenstrual issues, polycystic ovarian syndrome, and more. Magically, sachets are placed inside pillows to allow the scent to carry the dreamer on astral travels. Don't worry, men, the estrogen can't hurt you through scent. The smoke provided by burning dried chaste tree berries as incense assists in meditation as well as feelings of peace and tranquility. Its associations with hearth goddesses Hestia and Vesta, as well as Hera and Juno, give it a link to the hearth and marriage. You can also call upon Hestia/Vesta to bless family life in times of strife. Moonstone is associated with familial relations and can be beneficial when attempting to deal with the many vagaries of familial interaction. Just ask Hestia to bless it, if you're comfortable doing so.

Brass Tacks: Practice Time

Another herbal smoke that bears discussion for families and encouraging love is basil. Basil is associated with Aphrodite, as well as other goddesses of love. Burning basil's love associations helps in times when strengthening an emotional rapport is called for and can be added to love incenses of all kinds. It is appropriate to use burning basil leaves as an offering to Aphrodite and other love goddesses to encourage loving harmony in families.

Take that protective energy that basil is known for and let it safeguard your home and family (whether chosen or blood) and get the things you need out of life. You can add dried basil to salts for strewing about for exorcism (see chapter 9). Evil can't abide basil, and as it happens, the smoke of dried basil burned in the home drives out evil spirits. Just ground and center, then sprinkle dried basil over burning charcoal and visit each corner of the house with the burning basil smoke. We'll go into more details on this practice in chapter 4. A sprinkle of dried basil in the corners of the rooms ensures they don't come back. We always have to work in the real world where we live as well.

Pomegranate is a charm for helping to restore work/life balance. So find a time to spend with a romantic partner or as a family eating pomegranate seeds and listing things you're thankful for, in each other, in having a home, etc. If pomegranate is out of season or unavailable near you, try making up drinks with pomegranate juice and telling stories of your times together. If it comes to light that there isn't a balance to restore and it might be time to move on and find a new job, anoint an aventurine stone in pomegranate juice and whisper the things you need in a new job to the stone. Then carry it in a pocket on your dominant side while you look at job listings and apply for new positions. Renew at the next full moon if needed.

Changing Seasons: Rites for the Passage of Time

You don't have to tell me that not every story features two happy parents and a picket fence. We all face challenges in dealing with our family past, present, and future, so here are some ways plant allies can help.

Negative Family Patterns

To change hereditary patterns, stuff a poppet (doll) with morning glory seeds and ask Artemis to help make the needed changes in the present and future. If you want to get really specific, write the needed changes on a small piece of paper and either stuff the doll with the paper or burn it. If you can, burn it with one of the herbs from the list of Allies to Burn to Banish Toxic Family Members.

Toxic Family Members

Combine any of the materials listed here to create a pleasing incense to prevent the toxic member of the family from rearing their head, or to help them to see their way to the door should they make an unexpected appearance. If they pop into your life, burn the incense as quickly as possible to banish them. Even if it's just a whisper or hint of a visit. Your own intention to keep them far away from your home will be a powerful fuel for that work. If you'd like to signal to the universe that they are never wanted, feel free to mix as many of these as you find pleasing to your nose, write out your intention for their permanent banishment, and make sure the smoke bathes inside and outside of the space if possible.

Allies to Burn to Banish Toxic Family Members

Angelica

Basil

Clove

Dragon's blood

Frankincense

Pine

Growing the Family

Fertility magic is a wide subject, worthy of its own book. Cypriots engage in an annual ritual where a designated family member uses the smoke from burning olive leaves to cleanse the entire family in a practice called Tutsu. It ensures the family is as fruitful as the olive tree the leaves come from and protects them all year long from the evil eye. Divination is performed using the burning coals after the smoke dies down. If you don't have access to olive leaves to burn, patchouli leaves also have a long history in fertility and love magic, as well as increasing feelings of protection and security. The Saturnalian associations can make it a good substitution for the divination as well.

Family Blessings

Anytime your house feels in need of a blessing, burn true bayberry candles. Bayberry is a fruit found in the original colonies and carries a natural wax coating. The colonists would boil the berries, and when the wax would rise to the top of the pot, they would scoop it out to make candles with. It's traditional to burn a pair of candles on the winter solstice to bring luck for the next year. "A bayberry candle burned wick to the socket, puts joy in the heart and gold in the pocket," goes a traditional rhyme.

Overcoming Anxiety

For anyone dealing with anxiety, especially in family matters, there are a number of essential oils that can be soothing to diffuse in your home. Be sure to research them to make sure they don't interact with your current medications and aren't otherwise contraindicated.

Antianxiety Essential Oils

Bergamot

Cedarwood

German chamomile

Lavender

Marjoram

Melissa

Neroli

Petitgrain

Roman chamomile

Rose

Sandalwood

Sweet orange

Tangerine/mandarin

Vetiver

Ylang-ylang

     Sacred Smoke

Featured Herb: Sandalwood

Santalum spicatum.

Australia. Burned in rituals for healing, protection, love, harmony and balance, psychic growth, fidelity, purification, and forgiveness.

Sandalwood has a history of spiritual connection. No matter your religion or spirituality, sit with the spicy, woody, sweet, and warm sandalwood smoke and contemplate the state of your faith surrounded by its comforting aroma. Is there room for improvement? What can you offer to those around you? Please note: Sandalwood (*Santalum album*) has become a threatened species and there are poaching rings and frequent counterfeiting, especially in the essential oil distillation processing. To ensure you have an ethical product and are not supporting wood poaching, be sure to source your sandalwood from Australia. Currently, the largest sandalwood farm in Australia is three times the size of France, and Australian farming regulations for tree harvesting ensure that it is done with the continued health of the planet in mind.

Featured Resin: Opoponax

Commiphora erythraea.

Somalia. Also known as sweet myrrh. Centering, hex-breaking, prosperity, transformation, astral strength, awareness, opening blockages to your best self and blockages to material objects (house, cars, etc.), protection against negativity, and exorcizing toxic people.

These trees bear a resemblance to *Euphorbia milii* var. *splendens* or the crown of thorns plant in both their leaves and thorny branches. Both are subtropical plants, but the sweet myrrh grows three meters or nine feet tall. The preservative nature of all resins is well known, but sweet myrrh and its cousin *C. myrrha* were used in embalming in the Middle East.

Are false friends feeling fine? Banish them with some sweet-smelling, earthy, and warm opoponax gum and a smile. Just hold a few granules of resin in your dominant hand and say the person's name over the resin. As you burn the resin, see them disappearing from your life forever. Sweet myrrh carries away sorrows too, so you can let them go without sadness. Sweet myrrh can be burned in meditation to help induce feelings of serenity and connectedness to the universe, the divine, etc. To consecrate a new prayer corner, altar space, or other religious space, burn opoponax resin to sanctify it to that purpose. Oils can damage wooden surfaces and strip the finish, so sacred smoke is more appropriate in this instance. Opoponax is also used to create a balance of power in romantic relationships.

4

Up, Up, and Away

Sacred Smoke for Purifying Your Home

Close your eyes. Go on, just for a moment. Picture your home from the outside, just as though you were standing out front. Imagine it in as much detail as you possibly can. As you work with this book, this skill of visualization is going to become more and more essential, and the more you practice it, the better you'll get at it and the better you'll be prepared for the heavier lifting at the end of the book. This is a book for beginners, but you won't be by the time you're finished reading it, right?

So, picture your home, no matter what the building looks like from the outside—apartment complex, house, converted factory space: it doesn't matter. Picture it at dawn. See the sunrise. Speed up the camera so that an entire day passes in a few seconds. Visualize the path of the sunlight over your home, and know where every spot of shade falls, down to where animals are likely to nest. Get to know the exterior of the building the way you know your hands. By being able to reach into your brain and build your home in your mind's eye, to be able to pick it up the way you would your phone, turn it over in your hands, and examine it, you can check it for flaws, cracks, or holes in the defenses of your home—once you set them up, that is.

We spend a lot of time running back and forth to work, school, the grocery store, and so many other places in our lives that we don't often remember to stop to look at the buildings where we spend a good portion of our time. Could you pick yours out of a line-up? Could you describe it to a sketch artist if it went missing? But you are saying, "It's a whole building, it isn't going anywhere." This is how we ensure that remains the case. We are going to keep our homes safe and secure when we aren't there to protect them.

When you have the spare brain power—and it is safe to do so—picture the exterior of your home. Do this whenever you are working on small tasks that don't require 100 percent of your attention. Practice makes perfect, and you need the psychic equivalent of muscle memory. Once you have gotten the hang of seeing what it looks like in your mind's eye, I want you to pick up the whole thing in your hand—like your phone, a ball, or any other small object—because we are going to be turning it over and around to get a feel for different angles. This is to ensure that you really know what it looks like from all sides.

Once you can throw this particular "ball" into the air and still know what your house looks like no matter how it lands, you're ready to start the real work of protecting your home with your sacred smoke.

Brass Tacks, Practice

Gather one or both of the featured materials from the end of this chapter along with your incense charcoal, burner, tongs, a windproof lighter, resin spoon (don't burn yourself), and anything else you think you might need. Use the tongs to hold the incense charcoal (remember, the saltpeter makes it light quickly and evenly, so you don't want to just hold it by the edges and hope for the best). Once your charcoal is lit (tip: if you think it's lit, you should smell a faint whiff of ozone), drop a single rosemary leaf on it to see if it smokes before adding more material. You don't want to waste more material if you have to relight the charcoal. Add more rosemary and/or dragon's blood once the charcoal is hot enough.

The next step is to open a window farthest from where you will be starting in the home. In the case of an apartment, you might open a window facing the west because that's the direction the sun travels, east to west. In a multilevel home without a basement, I might start in the attic and end up working my way out the door. The point is to get into each nook and cranny in the home in between locations A and B. Because I practice magic, I prefer to set my intention by working counterclockwise through my space when I'm banishing negativity, bad vibes, or energy I don't want in my area. You are giving anything nasty in the home an out while you are working by driving it to the open window, door, etc. You don't want to go through all of this work only to trap it in the corner for a week.

Walk through all the areas of your space carrying your brazier in a safe way that won't burn your hand while you bathe them in smoke similar to what you've done so far in chapter 2 with your body. If you can do this when you have the least amount of distractions possible, great, but I know that's asking a lot. Not everyone can drop what they're doing to run through an empty house with fire and smoke. Make sure you are getting into closets, showers, behind the mirrors in medicine cabinets, while still being observant of the burning materials.

I'm a modern practitioner, so during a recent house cleansing I did to banish a nasty spirit (don't try this at home, beginners' sage is *not* going to cut it), I used modern technology to give me a hand. Once I completed my journey from the attic to the basement, I stood next to the heat return for a moment to get the heating system to spread the smoke for me to make sure I had gotten it well into every room.

I chose rosemary and dragon's blood for this chapter because of the purification properties of rosemary and the protective aspects of dragon's blood. Using rosemary to purify a space doesn't just leave it a blank and empty vessel waiting to be filled, as with something like white sage. It leaves the space feeling serenely happy, content even. Nature abhors a vacuum, so you want something good to fill in the space, rather than leaving it neutral and empty, potentially waiting for anything that comes along to disturb that fresh, clean feeling. Pairing that with dragon's blood, resin from the dragon tree, means that protection is also yours.

One of the ways I make sure that the protection lasts longer than just the smoke by itself is to seal the home with oil after the smoke cleansing is over. Following the same route that you took to drive out anything in the house, anoint all of the windows, exterior doors, the water main if you can get to it, the backs of mirrors in the bathroom, a small spot in the corner of a mirror (mirrors are doors, too!) with a protective sign or symbol of your choice. It could be a star, an equal-armed cross, a circle—it's up to you. Once you get to the door or window you left open, say, "and stay out!" Shut the door and be done with it.

Making Anointing Oils

So what oil are we anointing all of these windows and doors with? There are lots of options. Since we're burning dragon's blood here, there are many brands of dragon's blood oil that make for a great anointing oil on windows and doors. Just be careful where you put oil on wood as it can damage the finish. You don't want to inscribe a pentacle somewhere it will leave a permanent mark, especially if you're not out of the broom closet. Other symbols that are appropriate are equal-armed crosses, spirals, and circles.

The Vatican uses olive oil to bless its candles. It makes a perfectly good blessing oil for things that are going to be used quickly, as one would in candle magic, but it will oxidize and leave a rancid smell behind if it sits too long and we don't want that lingering around the house.

Instead, you could make your own anointing oil pretty quickly—a magical pen we'll call it. Just grab a 10 ml roll-on bottle you'd find at the natural food store, or from an essential oil shop online, some jojoba or fractionated coconut oil (they both have an extended shelf life without worrying about adding preservatives), and the oil of choice. There are so many protective plants out there, but here are a few easy-to-find essential oils for protection you could come across:

Amber (piney, sweet)

Angelica (dark, herbal)

Basil (herbal, sweet)

Bay (woody, sweet)

Bergamot (bright, sweet)

Clove (dark, spicy)

Lemon verbena (herbal, citrusy)

Myrrh (dark, resinous)

Patchouli (dark, sweet)

Vetiver (dark, grassy)

Just choose one that smells the best to you and put a single drop in the bottom of the roller bottle. Then fill it the rest of the way with your jojoba or coconut oil. Put the roller ball in place and the lid on, and give it a shake. Why go for the best-smelling one? There are a few reasons: One, because if it smells good to you, you're more likely to actually use it. Two, your brain is going to tell you what you need right now, and that could change in the future. Three, if you have a negative association with a particular scent, that's an exercise for another day; don't worry about fighting with yourself over old wounds when it comes to the safety of your abode.

Once you feel that the drop is blended well, it's ready to anoint the doors, windows and mirrors, candles, and anything your heart desires. As an added bonus, at this dilution, it will be skin safe unless you have a particular allergy to the material. (Always do your research! *Blackthorn's Botanical Magic* has a thorough list of essential oils to avoid when pregnant and specific warnings for each oil regarding such things as epilepsy, diabetes, etc.)

Changing Seasons: Rites for the Passage of Time

A word on cleansing practices for the home: once we have started a tradition, it is easy to fall into a rut. I want to stress how important it is that once you recognize how integral it is to cleanse your space and you start doing it regularly, you make sure you vary how that practice is carried out. If you start stocking up on one material and only use one method, you run the risk of developing what I jokingly refer to as a magically resistant staph infection. Say you have an "oogy" monster named Bob move into your home without your knowledge or consent. Things start to feel off in the home, and so you begin with your herbal allies to try and get rid of the general negativity. You reached for the polka-dot plant for this job, and every month Bob sees you coming with your polka-dot bundle he laughs because Bob is immune to polka-dot smoke. If you aren't getting the results you want, you've got to change up the program. If you use rosemary one month, try fir needles next month, melissa (lemon balm) the month after. Eventually you'll find the ally that Bob isn't immune to.

If you want to draw in a particular energy, such as prosperity, fertility, or other blessings, the movements through the home would be clockwise to bring in those energies instead of banishing them. See chapter 5 for more information on herbs to use as well as spells.

Well-Being: Checking on the Energetic Health of the Home

Every so often, go back to that first exercise of picking up the visualization of your home and inspecting it. Turn it over in your mind's eye and examine it for cold spots, fuzzy areas, and things that don't belong. Negative entities can be hiding in plain sight and attempting to fool our mind's eye by trying to appear as cobwebs, boxes, or things out of place. Don't hesitate to investigate anything in your home to make sure it belongs. Practice opening the home the way a dollhouse splits in half down the middle so you can peek inside and confirm everything is okay in there.

Hierarchy of Smoke Allies

There is a hierarchy to this work, and it makes sense when you think about it. The energy of plants concentrates depending on the type of plant and plant by-product being discussed—flowers, seeds, etc.

Flowers smell nice, but they don't hold up under the weight of the heavy lifters to come. Burning mullein flowers has been used for clearing space as well as clearing chest congestion.

Leaves are stronger magic than their floral compatriots because they contain more volatile oils and have more energy to give to the working. Mugwort, for example, is a boundary plant, meaning that it can be used as smoke to cross the boundary between the worlds or laid down as a border around your property to enforce personal limits for unwanted visitors.

Roots and seeds are stronger than the leaves because they form the foundation of the plant and are the basis of the network for the plant's ability to care for itself—the plant's "brain." Gingerroot has the fire necessary to burn away the ties that bind something to our homes that needs removing.

Wood allies are even farther up the food chain. These contain the life of decades' worth of the tree's knowledge because in almost all cases the entire tree must be harvested to procure these beautifully scented woods. Now that we're in an age of responsible stewardship, we are aware of endangered trees like sandalwood (*Santalum album*) being poached, so Australia has stepped up its game and increased its standards. The largest sandalwood farm for Australia's *Santalum spicatum* is now three times the size of France. For every tree that is harvested for essential oil, three more are planted.

Resins are the king of all smoke rituals, and the first to come to mind is usually frankincense. If an energy wasn't affected by the lower rungs of the plant kingdom, it stands a good chance that a resin will do the trick.

People often ask me why frankincense essential oil is so expensive. Once the seed has been planted, and a sapling starts growing, it takes twenty years for a tree to begin producing its signature sap that then needs to be dried and then turned into an essential oil. That's twenty years of paying the mortgage, paying for labor, keeping the lights on, and watering and caring for the trees while still feeding your families. Keep that in mind the next time you balk at the price.

Featured Herb: Rosemary

Rosmarinus officinalis.

United States. Burned for consecration, purification, protection, knowledge, concentration, courage, creativity, and blessing.

Rosemary is associated with those who have crossed over and messages, so if you are missing loved ones who are no longer with us, burn rosemary while talking to them, and the smoke can carry the message across. This herb has a bite to it that lingers sweetly. The herb also brings happiness and harmony to those who encounter its smoke. That harmony also manifests in banishing nervousness and boosting mental energy and creativity.

Sacred Smoke

Featured Resin: Dragon's Blood

Dracaena draco, D. cinnabari.

Sumatra. Heaviest of the heavy lifters, returns all space it touches to absolute zero—not good nor bad.

Once you burn dragon's blood, there will be nothing left, not even spirits. Make sure to fill the void with beneficial feelings, as nature abhors a vacuum. This resin is used for protection, consecration, and purification, also power, banishing, and is aligned with the crown chakra. It is attuned to the energy of fire and the planet Mars. Smolder a small chunk of this dark red resin to protect your home on those nights when it feels like something just isn't right even if you can't put your finger on it. Dragon's blood smells dark, warm, and sweet—almost like cherries or musk.

Spells Using Incense

Dragon's Blood Incense and Sage, Oh, My!

W hen I was beginning my practice, the first thing I'd do when I picked up a new book was flip to the table of contents, find all the spells, and go straight there. After all, what was the use of learning all this beautiful, empowering stuff if I had to sit through all the *other stuff* just to get there? So I'm a Sneaky Teacher (TM) and make sure I put spells and other good things throughout the entire book. (Insert evil laugh.)

Then why do we have a whole chapter right here dedicated to spells? There are a few reasons: A) Everyone deserves to enjoy some of the *fun stuff*. B) Magic has so much baggage attached to it I wanted to have a chance to talk about it in its own section without having to look at it through the lens of another topic. C) Everyone has to start somewhere. If you read about magic and decide that it's not for you, we're still cool; we can still hang. I'll even bring the tea. Even better, you can always still cleanse your space and work on your own life with all of the other techniques discussed in this book even if you decide that the magic part isn't what you're into.

What is magic? That is a huge question and it's a small one. Nothing is ever easy, and sometimes there are paradoxes—man, I have baskets of them.

People have been using herbs, plants, and more as incense, in magic, and in many other ways since we've had people. So, how do I define magic? I like the old-school Aleister Crowley definition: "Magic is the act of causing a change in accordance with Will." As in the story I shared in the introduction, it isn't about getting credit for causing the desired change; it's the existence of desired evolution. After all, anything that doesn't change dies.

More than that, magic is agency. Magic gives us the ability to alter our circumstances. It is the mantle we wear to give rise to a new world, whether personal, spiritual, or otherwise. We can perform spells to gain new jobs, empower political change, strengthen ourselves to make personal advancements, and so much more.

Want to learn more? Let's dive into some practice then.

Brass Tacks: Meditation

Those visualizations we've done in earlier chapters—of the body, family members, and our homes—those are the precursors to magic. In magical endeavors we need to be sharp on those skills of picturing things clearly for one important reason: you have to have a clear and present result in mind before the work or you have already started with muddy waters. Remember: it's called *practicing* magic for a reason. Just like with any skill, you have to *practice* it to get good at it. So make sure that you are taking the time needed to prepare yourself for the work at hand. I am also using the word *work* very intentionally here: this is fun—and it is meant to be—but it is work.

In order to start flexing those muscles, it's time to find a comfortable place to sit, and we're going to meditate. I promise it'll be (mostly) painless. Forget what you've seen on TV or read in a book. It's pretty impossible for social animals to totally blank their minds, so most people tell themselves they just can't do it and give up before they've even started. We're going to break all the rules. We're going to use all the building blocks we've set up so far. Don't think of this as a repeat of earlier material; now is the time to dig in and practice to be effective.

I.   **First, get into a comfortable position.** Some people want to be sitting, some lying down. Make yourself comfortable or your "monkey mind" will keep you fidgeting rather than getting on board the meditation train. Some people can't stand the thought of being alone with themselves, so they'll fidget rather than allow themselves deeper into the meditation. If you need pillows, blankets, incense, music, silence, the Doobie Brothers—whatever—it doesn't matter. You don't need to justify your accoutrements right now; you're just figuring this out. As you get the hang of this, you'll need fewer things, but in the beginning, your anxiety/desire to do it "just right" will tell you all that stuff is essential. (It's not—only you are, FYI.)

I was trading tarot readings with my best friend Laci one day a few years ago in her stone cottage. She is a massage therapist and had the radio set to some kind of New Age bell music. When the time came for me to read cards for her, I had to get up and change the channel. It was too distracting. Soon, the soft strains of Foghat's "Slow Ride" started to emanate from the speakers. This sent my dear friend into a fit of loving giggles. "I've never heard anyone read tarot to classic rock before," she said. The things that work for you just do. They don't have to work for anyone else—because you are the one operating.

2. **Center yourself.** Take all those scattered parts of yourself and file them away inside. There's no need to analyze them or let them bother you. They don't have any weight here; nothing does. You're gathering energy, nothing more. Pull power from your toes, legs, fingers, arms, and that brain (!) and ball it all up in your chest to deposit into the ground. Anxiety, fear, restlessness, all of these things can cause excess energy that leaves us spinning our wheels and going nowhere.

3. **Ground yourself.** Take big, amazing, deep breaths. Your body isn't going anywhere if it thinks it's starving for air. Make sure you're savoring each breath; don't just gulp down air because I'm telling you to. Create the persona of a sommelier and pretend you'll have to report back on the bouquet of the air around you when you're taking these great grounding breaths. Inhale slowly through your nose. Feel it tingle way back in there where you're smelling the air around you. (My writing desk has shelves of

essential oils surrounding it like a perfume organ, notepads for my research materials, and index cards for permanent notes that get stored. When I'm grounding, I notice the paper smells like real vanilla from the chemical breakdown of the paper-producing vanillin.)

You may even find yourself yawning when you ground because your body is trying to fight to regulate the big, deep breaths you're taking, and that's okay too. It doesn't mean that you've suddenly worn yourself out, just that your body is used to existing on the shallow breathing that comes from the top of the lungs, and when it comes time for the full belly breathing that you're giving it, it's going to take a minute to enjoy them.

4. **Start to visualize.** This is the part that's easy to begin but can take a lifetime to master. Pick an object—something that you see every day, have seen your whole life, and you would know in a heartbeat in a pitch-dark room if your life depended on it. An apple is a popular suggestion, but I think you can do better. When I was teaching this in a class recently, a student suggested their cell phone, but those change every few years and are obsolete before you know it—heck, my cell phone was outdated when I bought it.

So, pick your object and sit with it in your mind. If fruit is your jam, hold it in the hands of your mind's eye. Breathe in the scent of it, feel the texture of the skin. Cut into the fruit or bite into it and hear the sound it makes. Taste it and engage every single sense. You know you're getting the hang of the meditation when your mouth starts to water during the exercise.

Brass Tacks: Spells

Many spells fall into a few general categories: love, money, and protection. In this section, you will find some examples of all of these in the hopes that you'll be inspired to create your own workings. Remember to write them down so you will remember what works and you can modify what doesn't.

The Witch's Pyramid

Before we get into the juicy bits, we need to look behind the scenes of magical workings. The Witch's Pyramid is a key to making sure that your magic continues to be successful and doesn't succumb to easy pitfalls. And the Witch's Pyramid is "To Know, to Will, to Dare, and to Keep Silent." This means you have to understand what you're doing, by reading books and doing your research. Then you have to exert your will, or have the magic to drive the spell. It's the tingle you get in your bones that says, "This is going to work." Then you've got to have the nerve to go through with it. All the wishing in the world doesn't amount to a hill of beans if you don't *do* the magic. And lastly, you've got to let the magic work without drawing attention to it—no posting about it on social media or calling all your friends to announce you did a spell to get a new love interest, a new job, or banish the jerk in 3B. There are a few reasons for this, and they all have to do with having faith in your work.

I. Publicizing a spell lets in all the doubts of people who don't believe in what magical people do. They're pouring buckets of water on your spark. Don't let them.

2. All that pooh-poohing can make you doubt yourself. Don't you dare. Nothing can kill your magic faster than doubt. If you start doubting yourself, don't even pull out the cauldron, honey. Save those herbs for a rainy day. Believe in yourself because I do, and I've been doing this a long time. I'll even write you a note.

3. Even your magical friends who love you and support you may have different ideas about magical workings, how they should work, and why. Even that small variable opens up room for doubt, and we've already talked about what the doubt monster does.

4. Even if your friends don't doubt you and think you can do it, they may see you with a different outcome, like wanting you to end up with their dorky cousin Chad—who you think is a toad—and you don't want to hurt anyone's feelings. No one wants to get caught in the middle of Chad and his creeper vibe and bad breath. Just say no.

A Couple of Practicalities

One of the most beneficial tools for magic is flash paper. It is gone in an instant, leaves no trace, and creates no smoke. Consider trying to find some for magical endeavors. You can write petitions on it, concentrate on them, consecrate them with the sacred smoke you've created, and touch the paper to charcoal or lighter flame and poof—it's gone in a flash. So think about replacing plain paper with flash paper where possible.

Unless otherwise noted, the following recipes are for equal parts.

Love Spells

Love spells have a contentious history in the magical community. Fantasy books and movies depict them like drugs that remove all free will and consent, but since affirmative and ongoing consent is so important, I want to talk about love spells as drawing the correct partner, who is still ready, willing, and able to consent to be with you.

FRANKINCENSE AND MYRRH BEGINNINGS

Supplies

Scissors

Paper (red construction paper is best)

Pen or marker (a red pen or marker, if you are not using red paper)

Frankincense resin

Myrrh resin

Burning equipment

Timing: Friday (love) or a new moon

These two friends go together like ketchup and mustard, and they're sold together just as often. In fact, people often tell me that they think they're one thing: "frankincensenmyrrh." The heart of most spells is sympathetic magic, and this one is no different.

Cut the red paper into the shape of a large heart. Start your charcoal burning, but don't put anything on it yet. On one side write all of your perceived blockages to happiness that frankincense is going to bust through and banish. Add frankincense to the charcoal and fan it with your heart. Make sure to pass the heart through the smoke. Less is more with resin; we don't want to smoke you out of your place.

On the other side of the heart, and only after you have finished with the first side (no turning back now), think of and write down all the uplifting, happy things in your life that you have attracted, all of your successes, and times you showed compassion for others. Now you can add myrrh to the charcoal. (It's okay if there is still some frankincense burning there when you do this.) Fan it with the heart, and make sure to get that gorgeous smoke on both sides.

Myrrh is compassionate. It is about endings, and it is therapeutic and protective. In this love spell, its work is twofold. It is about self-healing, so it's good for anyone: ace, bi-, pan-, hetero-, lesbian, or gay. And this literal and figurative clearing of the air shows the universe that you are ready, willing, and able to expose your true self to a new relationship, even one with yourself. You are prepared to be vulnerable, and you are prepared to accept help. It takes a powerful person to open up like this and be honest about it, to come up with things to say that aren't just surface level. Take that honesty and run with it. Be free. Nothing is sexier than someone who is open to being themselves and confident about it.

As for what to do with the heart now, that's up to you. If you think you need to keep it around to remind you of your intent, hold on to it. If you want to burn it, light it up. Do something that empowers you; you'll know what you need better than I.

PATCHOULI AND SANDALWOOD DIVINE LOVER —TO DIVINE THE FUTURE

Supplies

Dried patchouli

Sandalwood

Burning equipment

Timing: Saturday (divination) or the dark of the moon

Patchouli and sandalwood are both incredible allies in love spells. Patchouli is associated with love because it's an aphrodisiac in its own right. The earthy herb is also known to increase the power of spells it participates in. Sandalwood brings harmony and balance to the working and the relationship resulting from the working. Sandalwood is a calming wood, grants wishes as well as fidelity and honesty, and is another aphrodisiac.

Both of these plant allies are known for being utilized in divination as well. Sandalwood is so calming that it helps induce a trance

Sacred Smoke

state if you can still what yogis call your "monkey mind" and let it drift in search of the topic at hand. Patchouli, on the other hand, enhances clairvoyance (clear seeing) and contacting other planes as well as divination of all kinds and psychic protection while you're out in the ether collecting data.

So what now? Light the incense charcoal and make sure it's nice and hot. Sprinkle some dried patchouli leaf on the disk to be sure it's going before proceeding. Once this is burning well, mix one part patchouli to one part sandalwood, and put two good pinches onto the charcoal while you start your deep meditative breathing. You're looking to answer love-related questions you can see for your next love/relationship. "Where will I meet them?" "What do they look like?" "How will we meet?" Once you've given this technique a try, the featured herbs wormwood or mugwort can be attempted for a more in-depth look.

BASIL AND ROSEMARY MARRIAGE MESSAGE

Supplies

Dried basil (love)

Dried rosemary (marriage, memories)

Paper and pen

Burning equipment

Timing: Friday (love) or a full moon

If the time has come in your established relationship when you are hoping for a marriage proposal and you would like for the discussion to move in a more serious direction, it is time to signal to the universe that you are ready. Basil is an herb of love, sacred to Aphrodite, and of fidelity, fertility, protection, and wishes granted. Rosemary is an herb of marriage. It banishes nervousness and brings peace and strength.

When the charcoal is burning hotly, sit before it with pen and paper in hand and write out the reasons for marriage. It can be a long form, in the shape of a letter to yourself or your partner(s), or it can be a list. Let this exercise rejuvenate those loving feelings inside. Once your work is finished, add one pinch of each herb to the charcoal and allow them to start smoking as you close your eyes and meditate on the path your relationship has taken. Every journey has pitfalls, side steps, and detours. What have you overcome on your journey to be together? How can the two (or more) of you grow together in love and mutual support and admiration?

And if a proposal is meant to be, bless all of the rings in the smoke of burning cardamom pods before the wedding, preferably on a Friday or under a full moon; it'll strengthen the union.

CINNAMON SPICE OF LIFE LUST INCENSE

Supplies

    1 part ground cardamom (increase libido)

    1 part ground cinnamon (love, creativity)

    3 parts ground clove (love)

    3 parts ground ginger (energy, love, passion)

    Burning equipment

    Timing: Thirty minutes prior to intimate activity

Use small amounts in a well-ventilated area; nothing is sexy about coughing up a lung. Make sure not to go overboard with the cinnamon; it smells terrific burning, but in an enclosed space it can irritate the lungs. Use caution, especially with asthmatics and others with breathing conditions.

Prosperity Spells

BAY BUSINESS BRIEF

Supplies

> Bay leaves (confidence, attract money, good luck)
>
> Burning equipment
>
> Timing: Sunday (success) or the full moon

Bay leaves are ruled by Apollo, the Greek god of the sun, and suited to working for business matters from developing a business plan to magic involving gaining new customers, overcoming obstacles in business (such as loans and finding storefront locations), or getting ready for the sale of the year. Bathe yourself or your store in the smoke of bay leaves. I do this in my shop before Black Friday to keep it prosperous and bless it with good luck all shopping season long.

Bay is the energy of monetary transformation, so if you're in the planning stages of starting a business and need to get your credit in order before applying for a loan, anoint copies of your credit report with diluted bay oil (it's also a good luck charm!) by placing one drop in a 10 ml roller bottle and filling the bottle the rest of the way with jojoba oil or fractionated coconut oil as a carrier oil. Use your new "magical pen" to draw symbols that are important to you. Circles send the energy in all directions, and an equal-armed cross will create balanced energies.

ANGELICA AND CLOVE FINANCE FIXER

Supplies

> Angelica (success)
>
> Clove (luck)
>
> Burning equipment
>
> Timing: Sunday (success) or a new moon

Magically, both angelica and clove are fiery plants associated with the sun. If you have made some mistakes in your financial history and are working toward a brighter future, let these two allies lift your burden.

The earthy aroma of angelica allows you to learn to accept assistance while working toward gaining success. It can increase the power of spells, manifesting your desires, and is a strong hex-breaker, so if you have caused any wrongs in your past and have made amends, angelica will see to it that any leftover bad vibes fade too. Let the renewal of angelica heal those wounds. Angelica is also great for listening to your higher self, rather than the eight-year-old inside us that wants us to spend precious disposable income on frivolous things.

The warm spice of clove brings luck into the home and is also hex-breaking and purifying. Clove is aligned with mental powers, so it will help keep you engaged in ways to maintain your finances clear of debt.

Once your charcoal is burning hotly, scoop that smoke over your head first, and then work your way down from there. Consider working your smoky ritual in the place where you do your financial planning—your desk, the kitchen table, etc. You will associate the smell and the place where you did the work for a long time after the ritual is finished. Each time you walk by the space you will remember the working you did, and you will continue to make sound choices and put energy toward that goal.

CEDAR AND THYME AND CLARY SAGE FAST-CASH FOG

Supplies

Cedarwood (wealth, prosperity, success)

Clary sage (manifestation, prosperity, retention, material objects)

Thyme (courage)

Burning equipment

Timing: Friday (wealth) or the full moon

This blend of earthy scents has what most fast-cash incenses don't—a grounding in the long term. By using stable, earthy plants, you manifest your cash quickly, but you won't blow it on inconsequential items and need to resort to another money spell in a week.

As with our other money spells, work your magic near where you deal with your financials so that your working is rooted in setting up good financial decisions and long-term goals. Feel free to pass things like checkbooks if you use them, credit reports, your wallet, purse, and individual credit and debit cards through the cleansing sacred smoke.

When you are done, put a piece of the cedar in your wallet to attract money from now on.

Protection Spells

LAVENDER, FRANKINCENSE, AND BLACK PEPPER PROTECTION POWER

Supplies

> 1 part black pepper (courage, physical energy, protection)
>
> 1 part frankincense (banishing, protection, purification)
>
> 3 parts lavender (protection, peace)
>
> Burning equipment
>
> Timing: Saturday (banishing) or the dark of the moon

Lavender, an herb of Mercury, has numerous uses including protection and divination, as well as calming and soothing. It's associated with secrets—both retaining them and ferreting them out. Adding lavender to any potent protection powder will help calm the situation quickly and allow for seeing the problem serenely and clearly, which is sometimes difficult when we are faced with a personal security threat.

Frankincense's association with protection falls in line with its powers of banishing and purification. It works for protection because it also works to banish the issue at hand and provide blessings, while removing blockages to untapped reserves of strength.

Black pepper is the queen of mental alertness and physical energy. People were using black pepper thousands of years before energy drinks. It was said that you could put a leaf from the tree under your heel for physical energy that surpassed all reason. Its crisp and sweet smell provides protection by burning away threads of any threat to come your way—from uncrossing to driving away evil, as well as bad neighbors.

This blend of helpers will make sure that you have the protection you need. Burn it in the home and you'll still be protected on the go. If you have access to the essential oils, a similar blend can be carried in a nasal inhaler tube to remind you of your magical protection.

CARDAMOM, LAVENDER, AND LEMON BALM BLUSTER BUSTER

Supplies

> Cardamom (confidence, courage, partnership, purpose, strengthens unions)
>
> Lavender (harmony, protection, gentleness, stimulant, strength)
>
> Lemon balm (success, compassion, soothing emotional wounds)
>
> Paper and pen
>
> Scissors
>
> A square of fabric
>
> Some thread

Burning equipment

Timing: Tuesday (conflict/victory) or the dark of the moon

We have all met people who for some reason (usually unknown at the time) are hell-bent on making our lives miserable. We are usually told they are "all bark and no bite." Rather than add any more fuel to the fire, take a step back and try this blend first. As with any magic, make sure you are also working in the real world and document interactions with this person for later just in case things escalate beyond your control and you decide to take further action.

Cardamom, otherwise known as "French cinnamon," is great for boosting concentration and confidence in both your magical ability and your own protections. Lavender is going to help you find the strength and chill to deal with this blustery person without losing your cool. Lemon balm (also known as melissa) is used for compassion both from you for the bully and from the bully for you—soothing the emotional wounds that made them so ready to lash out—sociability, successful magic, and sympathy. Melissa is also a soulful herb that helps us process emotional trauma and concentrate on the work at hand.

Create a blend of herbs at hand with equal parts, and if you have a mortar and pestle, give them a gentle grind to incorporate them all together.

Now with your charcoal burning hotly, add a pinch of your blend to it as you get started with your pen, paper, and scissors. You are going to draw a gingerbread figure to represent the bully in question and cut it out. Once the figure is free, write their name (if known) and as much biographical data as you have (date, time, place of birth, middle name) to link the doll with its owner. Make sure to give the doll a deactivation date, between a month and six months from now, depending on how long you want the spell to remain active. You can always repeat the working later.

Then detail the harassment you have received in the past, whether it is snide "mommy wars" comments at the bus stop or remarks about your wardrobe on campus, street harassment when you are walking to work, or something else. Fill the opposite side of the paper, even if you write over other words and it becomes illegible. (If harassment involves following, stalking, and other threatening behaviors, call the police and add the boundary plant mugwort to the mix so the bully can't find your home.)

Once the story of the paper poppet is complete, put the poppet onto your fabric. Grab another pinch of the offertory herbs and place this on the poppet in the neighborhood of the stomach area. Fold the arms and legs over the herbs as though it were hugging them. Fold the head over next so they can hear what the herbs have to say. Make the poppet as small as you can before tying the bundle closed with the thread. Pass your new charm through the smoke of the burning herbs.

Carry this packet with you until the problem passes or until your deadline date is reached. Burn it, bury it off of your property, or if you used natural fabric and thread, cast it into a swiftly moving body of water and don't look back.

DRAGON'S BLOOD, COPAL, AND SAGE SPIRIT SCRUB

Supplies

Dragon's blood (protection, power, banishing)

Sage of choice (cleansing, consecration, protection, purification)

Copal (protection, exorcism, dispel negativity, peace of mind)

Burning equipment

Timing: Saturday (banishing) or the dark of the moon

This is a little different from the other workings thus far. These ingredients are going to be used in succession, rather than as a blend.

Dragon's blood resin is the strongest of the heavy hitters. A Mars resin, associated with fire, it burns everything to ash and leaves no spirit trace. Dragon's blood is associated with power, protection, and the cleansing provided by removing any thread of curses, hexes, or jinxes. The void left behind is neither positive nor negative, so we'll have to fill that when we are done. Make sure to cleanse the whole person or space afflicted.

After the dragon's blood has burned away, grab the sage (I like *Salvia leucantha* for its soft woolly leaves and warm, sweet smell) and place a leaf or two on the hot coals. Cleanse the person or place in need. Sage is attuned with consecration and provides harmony, peace, and protection. Sage also encourages strength, spiritual growth, and wisdom.

After the sage has finished, add enough copal to your charcoal to complete the working, for dispelling negativity, giving peace of mind, increasing the power of the spell, protecting those involved in the working, and sealing the door against any malefic spirits intent on returning. So mote it be.

Well-Being: Checking on the Energetic Health of Your Spells

How do you know if your magic is working? The easiest way is that you get what you wanted. The less obvious ways can be harder to judge. Divination is helpful, but not always so simple for a beginner. Did you cast a love spell looking for the perfect partner and make it so specific that the person couldn't possibly exist? (Thanks, *Practical Magic!*) Maybe you haven't really committed to the idea of dating yet and you are protecting yourself. Are you so anxious for a new job that you are checking the results of your work every five minutes? Don't let financial stress make you doubt your magical prowess and undo all your good spellwork.

So, what *can* you do?

1. **Do the real world.** Go meet people. Get out. Network. Whether you are trying to find romantic partners, get a job, seek out a new housing situation, or solve a number of other problems, meeting new people can introduce new faces and lead to the "I know a guy" guy.

2. **After a moon cycle, try again.** After twenty-eight days, have a do-over. Maybe you weren't on your A game. Maybe the moon was void of course (between signs). Maybe something was retrograde. Maybe you zigged when you should have

zagged. No matter what, you've been patient long enough. Give it another shot. Wash your face, take a deep breath, and try again.

3. **Reevaluate.** Think about changing up your strategy. Is that really the job you want? Do they deserve you? Can they pay you what you deserve to be paid? Do you have the time or the emotional resources for a relationship right now? If you can't keep a goldfish alive, the answer is probably no. Are you managing your finances, or are you playing catch-up every month? Is there a better way to handle this than a spell? Does your bank or local community center offer financial literacy training? Consider resetting your intention to come at your issue another way.

Sacred Smoke

Featured Herb: Wormwood

Artemisia absinthium.

England. Cleansing, banishing, improving dreams, calling spirits (especially at Halloween), love, protection, breaking the powers of a spell, and psychic abilities.

Wormwood has been burned with sandalwood to allow one to see beneficial spirits of the dead. Wands of wormwood, with a sprig of marjoram and thyme added, can be smoldered to anoint yourself with smoke before bed to dream of the face of true love, especially effective the night before Saint Luke's Day, October 18, or on a Friday night. Wormwood smells herbal, with almost an anise bite to it.

Featured Wood: Palo Santo

Bursera graveolens.

Peru. Aromatic and woody, this balsamic tree lends a peaceful air wherever it is burned and a sense of optimism and clarity. Great for relieving stress and tension.

This name means "holy wood," and this tree is the source for the South American copal resin, not to be confused with copal. Copal is expensive to import here, and this resin is readily available and has a similar smell and properties. Traditionally only the fallen branches of this revered tree would be used, but as popularity from the outside world has increased, so has demand. Unlike some allies that chase away all spirits, palo santo's holy reputation banishes only evil spirits and encourages helping spirits. This incredibly dense wood is difficult to keep lit, so having a fire source handy is recommended. Even Dogfish Head Craft Brewed Ales uses palo santo. They have a two-story tank in which to age their palo santo beer, and this gives it a legendary dark flavor reminiscent of the resinous source, imported in partnership with the indigenous peoples of Peru.

Rock and Roll Lifestyle

Adding Crystals to Up Your Game

Something we have yet to discuss is another earthy ally available in many places: stones, crystals, and gems. By adding stones to your workings you ground your intention in the long term. Once the smoke dissipates, it is easy to forget that anything was done at all, but by carrying a stone with you, especially one that has been bathed in the smoke of a blend you have created yourself, or during one of the spells in the previous chapter, it becomes a literal touchstone that can anchor you to the magic you have created. Every time you touch that stone you are reminded of the magic; it reinforces the working done and refocuses your mind on that intent. Let's talk in terms of *stones* as a broad topic, because the difference between crystal and gems is pretty particular. All gems are crystals, but not all crystals are gems. Think of it in terms of animals. All frogs are toads, but not all toads are frogs. So we'll just stick with stones for now. I've chosen some very common stones that will be easy to find, relatively inexpensive (at the time of printing, that is: a stone's status is always subject to change!), and available at most witchy/New Age gift shops. With a few stones on hand, and at least one of each color, you will be ready for just about anything you want to enhance with earthy correspondences.

A note on wearing these stones: keep it simple. Think of each of these stones as a radio station. If you're wearing every one, you either have a symphony or an entire electronics department worth of alarm clocks going off at once. Choose wisely. They don't have to be set in jewelry to be worn: tuck them in a pocket, a sock, or a bra. Just try to get them as close to you as you can. Having them in your purse works about as well as anything else in a purse—which is to say, it doesn't. Once something goes in, it takes twenty-five minutes and an act of God to find it again!

As with any new materials, start slowly. Pick one or two new friends and learn them inside and out. Read everything you can, and then add to your collection. Do not run to the rock shop and drop a paycheck on a fifty-pound bag of stones you won't even be able to name in a week, say what energy they will provide, or explain how to work in community with them. It is a waste of time and resources. Yes, they are lovely to look at, but you have better things to do.

Combining Stones with Smoke

Read about the stones below, and if one speaks to you, great! Then work with that stone and your smoke practice using the following steps:

1. Sit with the stone of your choice after it has been cleansed and cleared (passing the stone through smoke is the easiest until we get more detailed later in this chapter; if you can match the herb or resin to your intent, all the better) and close your hands around the stone.

2. Close your eyes and visualize your intention for the stone. Try to keep your language positive, in the present, and succinct. Instead of saying, "I don't want to be in debt," say, "I have everything I need." By programming your stone in this way, you not only let your stone know what you are looking for, you remind yourself of all you need to accomplish your goal, and every time you touch the stone or are reminded it is there, you are reminded of your intention.

3. Then keep the stone on you, as close as possible, as much as possible, until your desire manifests. If you are working toward a long-term goal, make sure to give the stone a nice touch up, both in cleansing (it will still pick up things from your snark-fest with a coworker to your frustration of sitting in traffic) and in your intention from time to time.

Stones in Order of Color

Black tourmaline

Always choose at least one black stone, as these are perfect for repelling hexes away from the wearer and protecting against negative energies. Black tourmaline is so adept at protecting the bearer of this stone that it can lead the bearer to the sender of the hex itself. Black tourmaline is so good at repelling hexes that, when worn regularly, it's pretty easy to see which people fall away from your life. In its raw state, it is easy to tell apart from the myriad of other black rocks because of its clearly defined black cleavage (those straight lines that run through it). The striations are so pronounced that, magically, this stone has a very stabilizing effect on the life of the wearer, even memory and thought patterns.

The grounding properties of black stones resonate with the base of the spine and the soles of the feet to form a stable platform from which to genuinely connect with the earth, sloughing away excess energy, scattered thoughts, and erratic patterns of behavior. It can even ground mild inflammatory responses in the body, including arthritis, acting as a pain-relieving agent.

Selenite

This stone cleanses other stones just by being placed in their presence, so it's no surprise that selenite is known for providing clarity of mind as well. If you are having a hard time with the material aspect of running a business, turn to selenite. It can clear the air, so to speak, and clear your mind. Selenite is also ready to lend a hand in the area of fairness in conflict. It provides cleansing of the energetic body as well. Selenite helps us embrace our inner flexibility to see each problem from both sides, making it possible for us to best judge a whole conflict without the burden of personal emotional attachment in the way.

A word of caution: In recent times, the popularity of selenite has led to unscrupulous online sellers offering "powdered selenite" for use in magic. This is very dangerous. Under no circumstances should you purchase this material. Selenite is a form of gypsum, and in its powdered form the fibers can easily be inhaled and "can irritate the nose, throat, and lungs causing coughing, wheezing and/or shortness of breath. High exposure can cause a headache, nausea, vomiting, coated tongue, metallic taste, and a garlic odor of the breath" (New Jersey Department of Health and Senior Services).

Garnet

Garnet is used to cleanse the physical body of energetic flaws that lead to ailments. In the fifteenth century, garnets were ground into drinks of nobility because they were thought to neutralize poison.

Garnets remind each person of a commitment of self, that no matter how loving and devoted you are to others, you still have to see to your own needs too. As we are reminded during in-flight instructions, you must put on your air mask before helping others. You can't pour from an empty cup. Garnet helps recycle the energy we produce into mental and physical "availability," meaning it regenerates and helps us find our second and third wind without the need for energy drinks. Garnet is a very protective stone, the fire within providing a flaming shield around the wearer. Think of it as a passive defense system that burns up negativity on contact with your aura.

If you have had issues in the past working through emotional blocks, pick up a garnet. Meditating with garnet and identifying and listing those issues while working with garnet will help break down those walls.

Carnelian

This red-brown stone is accomplished at stabilizing (brown) the "red" emotions of rage, hate, anger, and fear. It is attuned with Leo and therefore can help the bearer if you're looking for a place in the universe or the spark that you bring to the web of life. Most red/pink stones are attuned to the energy of love; it is just about understanding what filter each individual stone puts on that wavelength. Carnelian reminds us that each person has some love to give, and the brown in the carnelian provides stability for loving energy applied to home life and the nurturing needed there.

If used in directed crystal massagers, points, or other shapes, it can be a potent cleansing aid for other stones that may have been exposed to negative energies or people (especially beneficial for retail work around the holidays, office jobs around bonus time or employee evaluations, or other contentious interactions). Also effective against psychic attack, the carnelian is a passive defense system that merely returns the energy from whence it came without any need for conscious thought.

Carnelian is incredibly useful in balancing all the energies of the body. Rather than grounding all the body's energies like hematite (not recommended for those who enjoy a relationship with the Good Neighbors or the Fae, as it is an iron ore), carnelian provides balance to everything and hopes for the best. This includes emotional balance, encouraging helpful communication in times of strife with friends, family, colleagues, and even enemies. If rational, mature, and beneficial communication is paramount, reach for carnelian. The mental stability can't hurt either.

Citrine

Along with selenite, citrine never needs cleansing. These are the only two stones on the planet that don't. Their energy signatures align in such a way that they don't require it. Selenite is self-cleansing because of its chemical makeup, its crystal matrix, and a radiant connection to the moon. It repels negativity. Citrine, however, transmutes negativity and releases it like a magical HEPA filter.

Since citrine carries the energy of the sun and is associated with Leo, it is great for magic involving protecting the resources—think gold!—that you already have. Tuck a small piece of citrine in your register, cashbox, purse, or wallet to make sure your resources keep producing for your business. It ensures that not only do you continue gaining new customers, but you hold on to the money that comes in, deflecting unforeseen costs due to mishaps, accidents, or costly repairs—again due to citrine's habit of bringing in negative energy and turning it into beneficial energy. If you have questions concerning the direction of your business, meditation with citrine can be of benefit.

Citrine's balancing act can also work for the energetic equilibrium in the human body, ensuring that people have the correct balance of yin and yang energies in their bodies as well ensuring that they are ready to step forward as magic workers in control of their personal power.

The solar aspects of citrine and that Leo connection also form a crucial link to the primal brain, ensuring personal endurance in times of stress and even danger. It helps with the higher understanding that we must act to save ourselves so that we can continue to keep others safe, happy, and healthy, whether those others are our children, families, or friends. No one has the right to harm you. In this role, citrine can help clear up questions concerning our own moral compass.

Aventurine

This milky green member of the feldspar family resonates with the heart so clearly that working in relationship with it is much like coming home, going to tea with a beloved relative, or coming in from the cold to a warm comforter. It works to gently disentangle old thought patterns from the heart space, even the back of the heart where old wounds like to hide, even from ourselves. If you will be entering into a potentially toxic emotional space, consider utilizing a technique you can practice beforehand to shield your heart with a breastplate made of aventurine. Simply visualize a thick, strong breastplate to protect you from the slings and arrows of overbearing family members, protesters, and abusive bosses alike.

Because of aventurine's heart-healing capabilities, it is a great stone for artists, actors, writers, and creative pursuits of all kinds because it helps us see the worst in people and work to counteract it without disempowering people along the way. It is ruled by Aries, so starting projects is no problem; it is the follow-through that may need some assistance. Aventurine can smooth that out too, though, since it is designed for keeping the mind/body/spirit as well as emotions all stable and working in unison.

Aventurine helps us see in others what we do not like about ourselves and then eliminate those behaviors in ourselves. With aventurine in our corner, we are always working to clean out the cobwebs that lurk in our hearts to be the best person we can be.

Lapis lazuli

At first glance this blue-and-white stone could be mistaken for sodalite, but just look for the flecks of pyrite in lapis to tell the two stones apart. Lapis lazuli is ruled by Sagittarius, and because this stone is supposed to be one of the first stones discovered, it is associated with increasing your insight and good judgment. Perhaps this reputation is one of the reasons it is discussed in so many ancient esoteric books and texts. It is said that merely possessing this stone gives you access to untapped power of the ancient world. Having been around for a while, I can tell you, magic doesn't work by osmosis. The stone does, however, connect your own spirit to the spirit of the planets. If you want to expand your intuitive abilities, lapis lazuli is absolutely a stone to develop a relationship with. It can help you expand your awareness, while making sure that you aren't overestimating your ability in those arenas.

If you are a member of a profession that encounters physical danger frequently, consider adding lapis lazuli to your protection regimen by putting a small chip of the stone in your protection anointing oils. Or consider a 10 ml lapis lazuli roller bottle, as this stone has a strong affinity for physical and psychic protection. For psychic protection while avoiding allergies, you could add a chip of the stone to a carrier such as jojoba without essential oils. This makes for a great anointing oil for large group rituals, where you may have participants with essential-oil allergies. With a Mohs hardness scale of 5–5.5, it will not dissolve in jojoba oil. (Always check on the hardness of stones before immersing them in liquid, as many stones such as jet, amber, or selenite may dissolve.)

Sodalite

Another blue-and-white stone associated with Sagittarius, this one has a little more color variation depending on its place of origin. Even though Sagittarius is the mutable fire member of the zodiac, sodalite acts as the stabler, more grounded and earthy member of its correspondences. Sodalite, unlike lapis, is rooted in the here and now on planet Earth, rather than in the stars. It wants to help you rationally think through your issues and come up with reasoned arguments for your problems. If you have ever dealt with brain fog, turn to sodalite to cut through the confusion. It will help you set a goal and go after it like an arrow toward your target.

Sagittarius's fiery aspect is particularly good for one thing, however: burning away mystery in your emotion. In every romance novel ever written there are confused characters who spend time wondering how they really feel about each other. If only they had sodalite on hand, the plot of the story would be much shorter. Sodalite clears away the cobwebs of confusion and shows us the light, and sodalite's resonance with the color blue connects it to the throat chakra to allow us to find our own way of expressing those feelings once we have figured them out.

The melding of the colors white (associated with the energy center governing our connection with the divine—after all, it's the one that sunlight hits first, and without sunlight, all life on earth would cease to exist) and blue (communication with the outside world) means that sodalite is the optimal stone for communication of ideas in sacred texts, of the divine, and who we are when we meld the two subjects of the divine and humankind.

Amethyst

This purple form of quartz is found worldwide, from the black-purple in Brazil to the pale lavender of the Ural Mountains, and everything in between. It is immediately associated with the third eye, intuition, psychic ability, and meditation. Amethyst is the ruler between the three parts of ourselves—the physical, emotional, and mental—as well as making sure our spiritual self is balanced and no one takes over. The resilience that is needed from all of the parts of ourselves can be enhanced with amethyst. It is the stone of the spiritual seeker; it helps to integrate new information when kept inside the aura during the learning process, whether we are learning to love ourselves one day at a time or understand complex ideas.

Amethyst has been used to facilitate the removal of toxic energies from the body left over from negative thought patterns and even overindulging in alcohol. (As always, stones are great for aiding in work you are already doing. They do *not* replace therapy, drugs, doctor's visits, and traditional medicine.)

Amethyst's connection with the aura, the third eye, and the interpretation of both makes it a beneficial stone for those who work with metaphysical ailments and etheric bodies. It is also the perfect choice for those looking at examining and removing internal patterns of behavior that no longer benefit from talk therapy, energetic work, visualization, or other means. It helps us find our way to the answers within our issues, rather than asking the universe to deliver the answer to us.

Quartz

This clear stone is the most prolific stone on the planet and has so many types it would take a lifetime to learn them all. Because it is all colors, there are so many types, shapes, forms, and variations they can align with any sign of the zodiac. Quartz generates its own electrical current by the pyroelectric and piezoelectric properties that most people are familiar with in quartz watches. Because of these properties, quartz is known as a magical battery and popularly added to magical workings of any kind to bring energy to the task at hand. Add quartz to candle spells when a boost is needed. Carry the stone when feeling low, slow, sluggish, or sick to shore yourself up. It works faster and longer than caffeine and without problems like heart palpitations, as the stone's natural tendency is to remain balanced with the bearer.

Keep a small bowl of tumbled quartz on hand for charging magical items like anointing oils, jewelry, and talismans before using. Just remember to run the stones under cool water quarterly or monthly, depending on how often the bowl is used, to keep the quartz clear of negativity. Simply see the water as coming from the source of all water as clean and sweet, visualize the stones clearing of negative energy, and say any words that feel appropriate at the time. It is also good to add a pinch of salt to the bowl if desired. (See the next section for cautions concerning salt.)

Well-Being: Checking on the Energetic Health of Your Stones

When working with stones, it is pretty important to make sure that you get to know each one and its personality. This is for a number of reasons.

1. **Health hazards.** Some stones are poisonous. Simply because a stone is lovely to behold and can be used magically does not negate potential lethality. Stibnite, cinnabar, galena, and others can cause health problems merely by handling them. With the popularity of gem elixirs and crystal-infused waters, be aware that using the wrong stones can also lead to a health crisis. I once intercepted a new student who had overheard another teacher and myself talking about gem elixirs and, without doing any research or attending classes on the subject, decided to start making her own, including one out of jet and amber, two stones associated with traditional witchcraft. Both are water-soluble, and jet is a type of fossilized coal. It would have made her very ill, and had her two-year-old gotten a hold of that water, there could have been a tragedy.

2. **Cost.** Damaging your stones can be quite costly either to repair or replace should the damage be permanent. During a busy day at Mystickal Voyage, a shop in Maryland where I once worked, a woman came in looking to replace a pair of selenite candleholders she had purchased just the week before. "You must have really loved them! They're a hot seller. I'm not sure if we still have them in stock. I'll check."

"Oh, no," she replied, "the faeries loved them even more than I."

"How do you mean?" I asked.

I came to find out that she had gotten wax on them and put them in the dishwasher. Lo and behold, when she opened the dishwasher after the cycle had run, she thought that the fair folk had absconded with her new favorite selenite candleholders. I had to explain to her that she had dissolved expensive stone holders because she thought stone meant "glass" or "dishwasher safe." While that may be true for some stones, it's not for all of them. Selenite dissolves in water and can be damaged by salt.

3. **Efficacy.** You want to make sure your stone relationship continues to flourish, and for that to happen, each stone needs its own space to work. Think of it like a water filter: after a certain point, the filter is still collecting debris, but at a much slower rate. To ensure that your stone keeps operating at peak efficiency, set aside time to check on each one and make sure

Sacred Smoke

it's operating the way it should. Use the same visualization techniques from chapter 3 to "feel" the stone and see if it seems dusty, sludgy, sticky, or muddy to your psychic senses. Other indications your stone needs clearing are that it will feel psychically hot even after rest periods. Think of how cool caves are underground: a healthy stone is one that feels cool to the touch.

How often? Wear stones daily, and cleanse them weekly if you're under duress or monthly if there's only a "normal" level of life happening.

How do you cleanse your stones? As I mentioned with quartz, there are some stones you can run under cool water, and they will be right as rain. However, do not do this with the soft stones like Shiva lingam, selenite, amber, jet, etc. You don't want to run stones under water that have fragile cleavage and can crack (fluorite, apophyllite). There are some stones that like to be buried in salt, but don't do this with any that end in -*ite* (selenite, hematite, covellite, howlite, etc.). I know for a beginner all of these rules run together and can be terribly confusing. So what can you do that will always be safe?

Sacred Smoke Rituals for Stone Care

1. **Decide on the intention.** (Is it cleansing of negativity, cleansing of a previous intention, a total reset, etc.?)

2. **Research and decide on the material to be burned based on the stone correspondences and your intent.**

3. **Carry out the cleansing or intention-setting by passing the stone through the smoke.** Feel free to say any words that feel appropriate at this time.

Featured Herb: Cedar

Thuja spp.

United States. Increasing clairvoyance; used for consecration, divination, financial gain; used in magic to gain material objects (houses, cars, etc.) and prosperity not limited to the finances and material wealth, physical strength, and success.

It is important to note the difference between prosperity and wealth. Prosperity is about the money to be comfortable now; wealth is the ability to maintain and grow it. Trees are in it for the long haul, so tree energy does not yield a quick fix for cash-flow issues. They are more related to long-term mutual funds. Cedar has a very sharp, signature woody scent.

Featured Resin: Copal

Protium copal.

Indonesia and South America. Used for exorcism, purification, astral travel to other realms.

Burn a small bit of copal resin to purify a home after a strenuous visit from someone who has overstayed their welcome. Note: This resin comes in different varieties, including black copal. Copal smells lighter with a hint of sweetness and an almost a citrus note similar to frankincense.

7

Plants

Growing Your Protection or
Farming It Out

I t is no coincidence that the featured herb for this chapter is an infamous weed. A *weed* is a plant that grows anywhere it was not planted and is usually pretty good at it. And mugwort does not need to be farmed, gardened, or really tended at all. If you have a small patch of this silvery member of the genus *Artemisia*, do keep a tight eye on it, or it will try to take over the garden. The lesson here is that with magical gardening, there is only so much we can control. We can love and tend the garden, but as with any project, there are pitfalls we cannot foresee. In such moments, all we can do is write them down and learn those lessons for next year.

For those of you swearing, like my beloved Sid, "plants only come to me for end-of-life care," fear not. That's where the Farming It Out part of this chapter comes in.

Why grow your own plant materials? As we have already discussed, some plants get so popular they are overharvested. Growing your own for your own rites of smoke ensures you are not depriving someone else of their sacred plants.

Another consideration is the changeable nature of plants and their availability on the market as a whole. It is absolutely easy to walk into a grocery store in the United States and find basil already dried and available in sprinkle-top canisters. But what happens if your job requires you to relocate somewhere where that is no longer the case, where the nearest grocery store is either two hours' drive or even a plane ride away? I have friends right now that live in the desert, where their fall temperatures are a "chilly" 98°F outside. If you want a taste of home in such conditions, you are going to have to grow something inside in a tabletop hydroponic garden because nothing thrives at 135°F. So your circumstances may change in an instant, but your allies don't have to.

And How Do You Get Started?

Begin with a window box, a pot on your balcony, or a small space on the patio. You can get a bowl from the local grocery store with a few culinary herbs in it. Rosemary, basil, sage, and mint are all perfect plants to start growing for your practice. Bowls like these concentrate our efforts by limiting our focus to a few herbs at first. Learn everything you can about them. Use them to cook with, but also use them in candle magic, incense rituals, poppets, charms, and more. Dry the materials to burn over incense as time goes along, and get to know what your plants look like in all four seasons. There is a wealth of information available for these commonly used herbs.

Remember, when we learn, we retain 10 percent of what we hear, 25 percent of what we see, and 65 percent of what we do. So if you want to really learn it, get out there and do it!

If you decide to grow your own allies:

1. **Make sure you have the right tool for the job.** When it's time to harvest your plant materials, use nice sharp scissors, shears, or clippers (depending on the thickness of the stem) that are only for cutting plants. Fiskars is a great brand I have worked with for decades as a florist and landscaper. (No, no one paid me to say that.) They make everything from scissors to saws. If you try to use scissors on a tree, you are going to hurt both the tree and yourself.

2. **Use the tool properly.** Make a clean, sharp 45°-angle cut so you do not damage the plant you are trimming. Studies have shown that plants know that they are being cut, so don't be a jerk about it.

3. **Honor the relationship.** Plants cannot continue to provide you with food, incense, or other materials if they die, so make sure you keep watering them, give them a little fertilizer on days you take material from them, and know that if you take too much, the plant may not recover. Saying nice things to your plants never hurts.

4. **Remember the law of contagion.** Picture a drop of blue food coloring in a glass of water: once the dye enters that water, it's going to be pretty difficult to get it back out intact, correct? It has "contaminated" that water. Ingredients are much the same. We only need a small amount of each material for our charm bags, etc., because they will still be lending their energy to the bag and no one wants to carry a three-pound charm. A little dab will do ya. You need not harvest an entire plant for magical purposes.

5. **Wear gloves.** Some poisons like wolfsbane can transmit toxins through your skin—no poison berries needed. Our skin eats 0.02-0.03 percent of everything we come into contact with through our pores—lotions, oils, etc. Make sure you are feeding it a healthy diet of not poison by wearing gloves while gardening.

6. **Watch out for irritants.** On the same note, make sure you know the Urticaceae family; all the urticating members (Latin for "to sting") of the nettle group leave behind red, burning welts that itch and last for days, and sometimes weeks. Then there are poison ivy, poison sumac, and poison oak, in the genus *Toxicodendron*, which produce the super-itchy urushiol. Make sure you know what all of these look like in flower and in each season as well. Just because poison ivy has cute little flowers doesn't mean they won't make you blister as well. People who believe they are immune to poison ivy, etc., may not react immediately, but they will later if the oils are not washed off

within twenty-four hours. Poison ivy remains active on clothing, fabrics of all kinds, and other surfaces for over a year, so make sure your gardening equipment gets washed thoroughly at the end of the season.

Sacred Smoke Allies to Consider Growing

Basil. Useful for prosperity, love, happiness, protection, ritual consecration, and hex-breaking. Herbal scent, slightly sweet. Dried leaves.

Bee balm (monarda). Love spells, prosperity, protection. Works whether sprinkled around the property or burned as smoke inside. This tall perennial is a favorite of butterflies, hummingbirds, and pollinators of all kinds. Useful for physical strength and success. Sometimes called bergamot, not to be confused with *Citrus bergamia*, the bergamot used in Earl Grey tea. Dried flowers.

Catnip. Ruled by Venus, used in restful sleep, love spells, and calming. Dried leaves and flowers.

Chamomile. Associations with Jupiter make it perfectly aligned for prosperity (just look at how many plants grow from a single seedling) and all gambling luck. Burn whole dried flowers over charcoal and cleanse any gambling charms as well as anyone going out for a night on the town. That crisp apple smell will help draw the gold to you. Smells like apples and sweet hay, used for beauty, meditation, peaceful home, and material wealth. Chamomile can be utilized for banishing negative energies in the home or within stones or other tools, as it has purification properties and is well suited for auric balancing. Those Jupiterian associations make it a great ally for small business owners who are looking to expand with a small loan, but don't want to expand too quickly. Anoint a copy of loan applications with diluted chamomile oil and waft it through chamomile smoke on a Wednesday or a full moon before filing the application. Dried flowers.

Dill. Ruled by Mercury, this herb helps you manage your own personal communication. Best friend of the office workers, it helps keep secrets and is great for psychic protection so no one is able to worm someone else's secrets from you. Utilize the seeds.

Geranium. Border your home with these flowers to keep the peace and add protection. Burn the leaves for a spicy clove-like fragrance and hex-breaking, inner growth, uplifting the spirit, and focused action if you are feeling aimless. Geranium is great for harmony in the home and renewing joy of those the smoke touches as well as fertility expressed both physically and metaphorically (through business, creative expressions, or other means). It is great for fast action when magic is needed in a hurry. Geranium can help heal emotionally wounded relationships and assist both family and romantic partners to "bury the hatchet" once both sides work toward a resolution. It inspires self-confidence and comfort in one's own skin as well as the courage to express the newly discovered self. Leaves.

Lavender. I know I've touched on this in a few places—so just grow it already. It's easy to cultivate, but takes forever to germinate from seed. If you live somewhere with a short growing season, skip germinating indoors and buy a four-inch pot of lavender to plant where you want it to grow outside. It wants good drainage, so if you live somewhere with a heavy clay soil, make sure to amend that with some peat. And remember it will need full sun to flower. You can burn the leaves and the buds. It's great for magic of any kind and adds a bit of sweet, minty, floral note to any smoke blend. You can't go wrong, unless you are allergic to it. (Don't feel badly, I'm allergic to roses, and my bestie Michael swears it's penance for some awful crime in a past life.)

Lemon balm (melissa). Sedative member of the mint family. It's an incredibly prolific grower with a sharp lemony smell. In aroma it helps inspire a joyful mood, but in food and drink it's a strong sedative. Avoid it if you are taking other sedatives as it could lead to an unsafe condition. Also good for rituals for letting go of old things, feelings, people, and situations. It is aligned with soothing emotional wounds. Burn dried leaves and flowers

while saying goodbye to that which no longer serves you. It's an herb of success, so if you have plans that you have your heart set on, burning lemon balm is a great place to start. It is also an ally of concentration, so if you need to block out distractions for the long term, ask lemon balm to aid you in your magic.

Marigold. These bright beauties align with the gold they are named for. Golden bars, success, wealth, and beauty, anything related to the sun and solar correspondences. These tiny solar generators can add a touch of solar magic to any blend with just a touch of a grassy note. Use flowers.

Peppermint. Planting mint is always debatable. If you want to have it, but not have it spread, cut the bottom off of a five-gal-

lon bucket, and plant the mint of choice inside the bucket so the runners will have a harder time seeking out new ground. I make tea, incense, strewing salts, and lots of other projects with my mint, so I have no problem with them stretching their legs. Their magic is consecration of space, joy, peaceful resolutions, psychic growth, renewal, healing, action, perception, clarity, mental acuity, banishing, change, overcoming indecision, cooling off after an argument, and relaxation. Mint could have its own chapter, and I cannot say enough kind words about this wonderful plant—seriously. (For more information on the magic of mints see *Blackthorn's Botanical Magic*.)

Things to Harvest
(Wild-Growing Allies You Could Have on Your Land)

Chickweed. It's the first green that comes up in the spring with edible, bright green leaves and tiny white star-shaped flowers. Grab a handful of this greenery and dry it. It's great for stopping gossip.

Clover (white or purple). Useful for prosperity, good luck spells, protection, intuitive ability, and overcoming obstacles. Try for the purple flowers if you can, as they're bigger and sweeter than their white counterparts and will burn better too.

Dandelion root. Adds a bittersweet scent to your smoke but is a powerful ally for creating deeply rooted luck. Dried root.

Honeysuckle. This vine is so stubborn it is just about impossible to get rid of. That stick-to-itiveness is going to work wonders for your magic. Honeysuckle flowers help it last longer and are great for magic involving dedication. Honeysuckle will also help your belongings stay rooted and keep thieves at bay. It's also great for things like prosperity, growth, and strength. Flowers.

Plantain. This stuff grows in most lawns all over the United States. Simply dry the leaves and add a small amount to other recipes; it's a bit bitter by itself. Because it is such a stubborn "weed" (you already know how I feel about that word), it's a great herb of resolve, transformation, and protection. It's another herb for stopping gossip. Are you noticing how many of the herbs that stop gossip all seem to be pretty bitter themselves? There is probably a life lesson in there somewhere . . .

Drying Your Haul

Once you have gathered your plants, give them a quick rinse to make sure they are free of dirt and particulates and pat dry. There are two main methods for drying herbal materials for use: traditional and in the oven. And there are also methods for microwaves, dehydrators, and even the refrigerator.

But first here are some tips for harvesting for drying:

1. **If you are harvesting something for its flower**—red clover, chamomile, calendula, etc.—aim for the first day these open to get the most volatile oil possible in the blossoms.

2. **If you are harvesting seeds,** the seeds should be maturing from green to brown but not releasing from their pods or flower heads yet.

3. **Try to keep an eye on herbs** like basil, mint, rosemary, lemon balm, etc., and pick them before they start to flower. Once the energy starts to go into the flowers, the herbs begin to lose some of their flavor and "life." Even if you are not ready to start harvesting mass quantities yet, just pinch the top of the flowering part and the plant will continue to produce leafy branches until you are ready.

Traditional Drying Method

Tie small bundles of herbs together at the base with a natural material (rubber bands will dry-rot and break down) and hang them upside down in a warm, well-ventilated area. This position makes sure that all the volatile oils that remain in the stem have returned to the leaves when the leaves are later removed after drying. Try and avoid the kitchen as the moisture levels from cooking, doing dishes, and 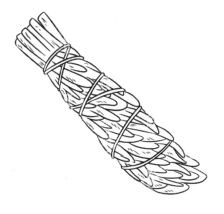 other activities can cause issues. Allow the bundles to dry for a few weeks (four to six depending on the season and climate). When they are ready, they will feel dry to the touch. Make sure to check the center of the bundle: if all of the herbs are not 100 percent dry, it can mold the whole batch if you put them away. Make sure the bundles are not too dense. The materials need air to breathe, otherwise they will become moldy and need to be composted or thrown out. Moldy materials are smelly and pose a health hazard when burned.

Once your herbs have dried, it will be time to strip the leaves from the stems and stored them in airtight jars for use at a later date. Feel free to powder herbs at this stage if desired; you will be able to store more herbs in a smaller space if they are already ground.

Remember, if it has been a while since you have pulled out your herbs, give them the pinch test. If they still have a smell when you pinch them, they are still good. For edible plants, always try for six months to a year, and for incense purposes, the pinch test is a great indicator. Once the plant materials lose color and scent, it is time to compost them and purchase or grow more.

Oven Drying Method

This method is more difficult because it requires a lot of monitoring. You will also need at least twice the number of sheet pans as you plan on using for herbs. Place a single layer of herbs on the sheet pan, allowing plenty of space for the herbs to wilt and breathe. Put the pan in the oven on as low a temperature as possible; the ideal would be in convection ovens that go down to 125°. Every so often place a second sheet pan on top of the first, flip it over, and place the herbs back inside the oven on the second pan. The cooler pan from outside the oven keeps you from having to turn the oven on and off in intervals as some instructions suggest.

The timing varies from plant to plant: for a leafy plant like mint it will put off a lot more water; something woody like rosemary won't put off much at all. You will know the plants are dry when the leaves feel stiff and drained of moisture but are still green. Don't let them brown or you will be losing all of the volatile oils that give the plant matter scent. If you burn a batch, compost them or use them for spell ingredients as they won't have enough scent to be used in incense. This is a time-consuming method, and I do not recommend it. Volatile oils are lost in the process, and while it will make your house smell great, the overall shorter drying time does not make up for the expenditure in labor.

Microwave Method

This one requires a bunch of paper towels, but those paper towels can be dried and kept for more herb drying, so they can continue to be reused if it bothers you that they are "wasted" on this project. On your microwavable plate, place a paper towel and the leaves stripped from the herb you want to dry. This will save drying time, especially with herbs with woody stems like rosemary. Feel free to cover the paper towel, as long as you don't allow the herbs to overlap or touch. Just make sure you can see a little of the towel around each leaf. Place another towel on top of the herbs. This is your steam catcher.

The most important part of this method is that the herbs start out dry; otherwise you are cooking the herbs, not drying them. If you have other methods or preparations you are doing, add this one last just to be sure. For those of you familiar with melting chocolate or cheese in the microwave, this will look similar to you. With the microwave on high, microwave the herbs for a minute, and rest for thirty seconds, and then microwave them alternating thirty seconds on and thirty seconds off for up to ten minutes until your herbs are dry to the touch. The most important part, once your herbs are dry, is to label them. There is nothing worse than going through all of this trouble and then six months later not being able to remember what these beautiful herbs are you harvested.

Dehydrator Method

The dehydrator method does what everyone wishes the oven method would do. The downside is the dehydrator requires some outlay for materials. It is worth it if you plan on using it for other projects—I make my own fruit leather with mine. Dehydrators go down to 125° and can run safely for hours without the monitoring needed for the oven. Yours can sit on the stovetop and run while you're at the store. It also has the circulation that most stoves don't have.

Refrigerator Method

This is probably the least labor-intensive and best for the blessing bundles that people are making themselves and putting photos of on social media. There are a few reasons that the refrigerator method works better than other methods. Your refrigerator has a built-in dehydrator that cycles hourly all day and night. The defrost cycle that runs inside the refrigerator and freezer will keep the herbs and bundles you make from molding, as well as fresh, crisp, and green from harvest to drying with the least amount of volatile oils lost. The best part is that since they are sealed inside the refrigerator, there are no damaging UV rays to fade the lovely colors of the greenery you've chosen to be a part of your bundles. I wrap my bundles in the half size paper towels that I reuse for each batch of bundles that I make for my own home. Just place them inside the refrigerator for a few weeks and they are dry in no time. (Again, these towels can be reused multiple times, so this method isn't wasteful.)

Farming It Out

Not everyone has a green thumb, and I understand that. Not everyone has the time, inclination, or space. I can remember living in a third-floor walkup with a north-facing window, no balcony, and no time to do anything for myself, much less another living thing. I had no desire to carry a bag of potting soil up that many stairs for an uncertain outcome. That's okay, I'm not judging. I have no room to throw stones.

And in such cases, one good solution is wildcrafting. Wildcrafting is the art of finding your materials in the wild and harvesting them for drying and later use.

A Few Tips about Wildcrafting

1. **Wear gloves.** Yup, I'm saying it again just in case you skipped the section for growing things because you had no intention of growing things, ever. Growing things like to keep doing that, so they will poison you if they can, or they will shank you if they can—just ask a rose. Invest in some thick leather gloves and a thinner pair that has been dipped in a rubbery textured material. You will thank me. Things with thorns require heavy gloves, but more delicate herbs will need a lighter touch.

2. **Invest in a good collapsible basket and sharp shears.** If you are serious about wildcrafting, they will wind up living in your vehicle all the time, and you will want them to take up as little room as possible.

3. **Never gather materials from a public garden without permission.** You don't know how recently they have been sprayed with chemicals for pests. You have no way of knowing if the material you are collecting is protected/endangered in the area if you don't ask. There are plenty of substitutions available out there, so please don't go to jail over spell ingredients. Plenty of books have conversion tables that can help you figure out an alternate method.

4. **Research. Research. Research.** Plants on the endangered species list are not going to have a glowing neon sign over them in the wild. You could be breaking the law and not even know it. In high school, I found an exotic looking orchid behind my home and wanted to dig one up for my mom for Mother's Day. I decided to look it up in a field guide and found out it was an orchid used by the Lenape to cure cancer but thought to be *extinct*. I called the local extension office to report the sighting and was excitedly told it was the subject of scholastic study as a possible cancer drug due to its history, and now they had a living specimen to work with. My choosing not to harvest this beautiful orchid is helping medical research.

5. **Do not take any herbs you've found in the woods internally—just don't.** Go to a doctor, trained herbalist, clinical aromatherapist, or other trained clinicians for such treatments rather than trying to heal yourself. There are simply too many look-alike plants for amateurs to eat from the woods. Horse nettle looks like green tomatoes, while Queen Anne's lace, also

called wild carrot, has a deadly look-alike in poison hemlock. Such confusions were responsible for the loss of 90 percent of the Jamestown colony in the winter of 1609 when they ran out of food early into that first winter and the settlers dug up what they thought were wild carrots but turned out to be poison hemlock and most of the settlement was wiped out.

Sacred Smoke

Featured Herb: Mugwort

Artemisia vulgaris.

United States. Cleansing, improving dreams and psychic abilities, establishing boundaries when sprinkled around the home or crossing into other worlds.

Light a mugwort stick (may be sold as "moxa sticks" in Traditional Chinese Medicine shops online) or burn this herb over charcoal as you walk the outside of the home to establish a border around the property to keep unwanted persons away. Mugwort smells strongly herbal, so use it in a well-ventilated area. It inspires lucid dreams and out-of-body experiences.

Featured Resin: Frankincense

Boswellia carterii.

Somalia. Used in religious rituals for 3,500 years for consecration, healing, balancing the chakras, protection, increasing spiritual ability, astral projection, and purification.

To bring your whole self into alignment, bathe in the smoke of frankincense. This resin has notes of citrus and a scent associated with Catholicism. To banish any unwanted energies in your life, tell it to frankincense; these sacralizing tears hold a strong banishing energy, and once you drop a tear onto hot charcoal and watch it melt into nothingness, your strength will rise and so will you. Many of the resins we have covered are associated with meditation, and the reasoning is simple: the deep, warm notes help calm and ground our thoughts and allow them to drift away into a meditative and introspective space. If justice is needed, frankincense is also the ally to turn to—it has qualities for banishing perpetrators, protecting the innocent, purifying space of evil, sanctifying victims of ill will and fear, and providing strength to make it through any ordeal. Frankincense will protect them from the evil attempting to return and will see that justice is served. Frankincense is also used in angel magic, so you can ask that an angel watch over those involved. Frankincense adds elemental power to any working, so if your working needs an energetic boost, consider frankincense.

Recipes

L et's not lose our heads. I understand the need for budgeting in running a proper household. There is no better judge for the needs of that household than you and any partner(s) involved. I suggest a technique called *simpling*. This means picking between one and three herbs and learning them inside and out. Use them for everything under the sun before adding one more at a time. That way you aren't overloading your brain and losing valuable information along the way. If you just go wild at the local New Age store and buy one of everything, by the time you make it home, you aren't going to remember what half of them are and none of what they are beneficial for.

WORDS TO DESCRIBE PERFUME OR SCENT

Animal. Any of the musky scents. Even the term *musk* actually came from the musk glands of animals killed to make perfume. These have mostly been replaced with synthetic musk, as anything that was animal-derived was priced out of the market. Old perfume and incense manuals will list ingredients like ambergris and civet. Ambergris was hardened whale vomit chunks (super appealing, right?) used as a fixative for perfume. Civet was a musk from the civet, a type of cat smaller than a lynx. They had to kill the cat to remove the gland, and several species of civet are on the endangered species list now.

Balsamic. This refers to any needles in the conifer family: fir, balsam, benzoin.

Citrus. Anything scented like citrus, but not necessarily citrus derived. Frankincense, for example, has a citrus note to the oil but is not related to the citrus family. Lemon balm is also sweet and citrusy but is a member of the mint family.

Earthy. Dark, viscous oils, relating to loam, soil, or earth, as in patchouli, vetiver, etc.

Floral. Any of the sweet scents associated with flowers, as in rose, jasmine, neroli. In incenses, these scents usually come from essences and will not smell the way a flower petal does. In most cases, the dried petals smell grassy and warm, rather than floral, when burned. Keep this in mind when adding flowers to herb bundles, as this will change the smell of the blend. The only exception to the rule is lavender, which acts more like a seed. Its camphoraceous scent will smell the same burning as it does growing.

Herbal. Herbs that produce scent along the lines of basil, rosemary, bay.

Resinous. Resins usually have dark, warm smells that can be musky in nature.

Spicy. Warm, flavorful scents that evoke feelings of caravans through the desert to trade goods like cinnamon, cardamom, and cloves.

Woody. The crisp smell of any of the whole woods, like pine, cedarwood, oud, sandalwood.

Incense Recipes

Before you dive in, ingredients here are given in parts, so they can be scaled up or down. A part can be $^1/_8$ of a teaspoon, or it can be a pound.

Also, always remember less is more. Both when you are starting out buying materials (a good rule here is to not buy more of each herb than you can use in a year) and when you are testing out your materials on the charcoal for the first time, don't smoke yourself out, especially if you live with other people who will either hate you for smoking them out too, or call the fire department without checking on you first. No one wants to have their door bashed in while they are in their robe because they had incense going.

Soul Flight Incense

Use for religious meditation/connection with gods and the universe.

   1 part basil (clear your mind, sweet smelling, herbal)

   2 parts cedar (can substitute cedarwood but use one part wood
      to two parts greenery; consecration, strength, success)

   2 parts lavender (calm, peace, strength)

   2 parts sandalwood (protection during meditation/astral
      projection, harmony, wishes, spirituality)

Grind together for best results before burning.

Love Lies Bleeding

Heals a broken heart.

 2 parts star anise (comfort in emotional times)

 1 part ginger (healing, comfort, love, improvement)

 3 parts lavender (balance, protection, clear seeing)

 3 parts sandalwood (intuition, honest assessment, love,
 protection, calm)

Mix on a Friday (Venus) if possible. The ginger can be a bit much the first time it is burned. So if the intended user has asthma, use ½ part and see how they react.

Temple Time

To consecrate sacred space.

 3 parts cedar (consecration, strength, success)

 3 parts frankincense (consecration, purification)

 1 part lemon balm (consecration, grounding, meditation)

Lemon balm does not smell as crisp and lemony when it is burning as it does in the tea you are used to drinking. It will be grassier and a little creamy. Feel free to finagle the amounts of this one a bit as all of the ingredients of this recipe are really gentle and sweet to work with and forgiving. Try to grind them together in a coffee grinder so that once you have the amounts finalized they stay that way. Otherwise, the heavy resins will all fall to the bottom of whatever container you choose to keep them in. If your container of frankincense comes as a frankincense and myrrh combo and the myrrh is along for the ride, it's no sweat. Myrrh is perfect for this application as well.

Cosmic Correction

Magical correction fluid for the universe, a do-over.

> 3 parts benzoin (hex-breaking, inspiration, knowledge, memory, peace of mind)
>
> 2 parts clove (dispel negativity, hex-breaking, protection, purification)
>
> 1 part patchouli (dispel aggression, hex-breaking, banish addiction, centering, protection, exorcism)
>
> 3 parts pine resin (divine assistance, purification of the aura, new beginnings, courage)

Everyone deserves a second chance if they are willing to admit their mistake and make it right. Sometimes you need your own ritual to mark the occasion. Patchouli loses its earthy aroma when burning, so don't worry, it won't smell like burning dirt.

Venus Remind-O

Remember your inner and outer glory.

> 2 parts pine resin (erase past mistakes, center, bring awareness, withstand adversity, purify aura, bring friendship)
>
> 1 part geranium leaf (awareness, healthy relationships, uplifting, protection, focused action)

1 part peppermint (antidepressant, clarity, healing, transformation, release, uplifting)

The Venus de Milo stands as a testament of time. She is an ageless beauty and a reminder that lovely qualities are within us all, no matter our age, gender (or gender fluidity), or sexual orientation. This is the first incense that is used as a process rather than an amalgamation. With your charcoal burning hotly, drop a piece or two of pine resin onto the disk and bathe in its sweet, healing smoke.

Remind yourself that everyone is beautiful and everyone deserves love. You are worthy of love, especially your own. Scoop another handful of smoke and wash it over your head as you remind yourself that you are worthy of friendship, especially your own. Feel yourself filling up and bursting with clean spring water until you have washed away any sense of inferiority or being unloved.

Once you have cleansed yourself of past feelings, blend the peppermint and geranium together and start adding these to the hot coals. All the feelings of clarity and protection they provide will uplift and transform you. They offer a focused and decisive plan of action whether you want to proceed to new romantic endeavors or not.

Weekend Retreat

Get that creative spark back.

2 parts benzoin (exorcism, harmony, peace of mind, wisdom, purification, prosperity)

½ part cinnamon (creativity, luck, uplifting)

2 parts rosemary (mental energy, peace, rejuvenation, strength, study, raise the vibration of the self)

1 part vanilla (relaxing, mental powers, passion, peace)

Creative types rejoice! Writers, artists, perfumers, and makers of all kinds—all have a reputation for needing a quiet getaway to get back to themselves for their work to come to fruition. This blend of cleansing and creative herbs generates a mental clean slate to clear out the etheric cobwebs without disturbing the creative process.

Cut open the vanilla bean and scrape the seeds into the mixture. They are very sticky and precious, so if you add them to the rosemary, they will stick in the mix better. Otherwise you risk losing these precious seeds to a bowl to be washed down the sink later. Make sure not to overdo the cinnamon as it can irritate the lungs, and do use this in a well-ventilated area.

See No Evil

See the truth in the situation.

1 part eucalyptus (restore balance, destroy disease, protect against angst, cleansing, mental clarity)

3 parts lavender (secrets revealed, harmony, gentleness, balance, strength, love)

3 parts sandalwood (awareness, freedom, emotional growth, balance, healing)

2 parts spearmint (clarity, healing, growth, purification)

This blend is designed to pull the rose-colored glasses off, but without being cruel. We all need the truth, but there is no need to be harsh to ourselves once we see things for the way they are. Our own situations can be enough to bear; there's no need to add any extra emotional weight.

With the different hefts and textures of these ingredients, it is best to give them a quick run through the coffee grinder if you have one. This helps the sandalwood and other materials burn at the same rate, but it is not strictly necessary.

All the members of the mint family lose a bit of their sharp minty-ness when they are burned, so feel free to experiment with the amount of spearmint when burning.

Bump in the Night

Use to banish monsters, ghosts, spirits, etc.

> 1 part basil (mental clarity, good night's sleep)
>
> 3 parts frankincense (consecration, purification, meditation, balance, uplifting, astral projection, protection)
>
> 2 parts pine resin (courage, defense, banishing evil, friendships, healing, hex-breaking)
>
> 1 part thyme (health, banishing nightmares, psychic power, purification, banishing sorrow, courage)

When we are young, it is important to find out we are capable of slaying our own monsters so that when we are older we can handle bigger monsters, bullies, illnesses, bills, and the innumerable list of things outside of our control. This blend of incenses purifies the space of any spirit of ill intent so a good night's sleep is at hand. Feel free to add a small piece of dragon's blood to this mix for the protection of dragons. Work with this smoke for any time you get a chill up your spine or the little ones have a monster in their closet. Remember to get them involved in the process of cleansing the room with smoke to empower them to take control of the situation.

Family-Tree Pruning

Use this incense in magic to banish toxic people in a nonharmful way.

> 2 parts cedarwood (strength, success, consecration)
>
> 2 parts lavender (protection, strength, love)
>
> 1 part marjoram (deterring harmful people from the family from returning)
>
> 1 part peppermint (banishing, change, dreams of release, overcoming indecision)

This incense is designed to nudge toxic people away. Sometimes those toxic people are family. This blend won't cause them harm; instead it helps them to understand that they need to change before they can be a part of your life.

Keep in mind that some people will never change and, if you are in a dangerous situation, you need to look out for yourself. If that person is in your home, the National Domestic Violence Hotline is 1-800-799-7233 or 1-800-787-3224 (TTY). If you are ages thirteen to eighteen and that person is someone you are dating, *LoveIsRespect.org* is designed for you, and their phone number is 1-866-331-9474 or 1-866-331-8453 (TTY).

Note: the cedarwood in this recipe is for stability, but if you only have leaves, double the amount used.

Business Blessings

Burn in workings for business finances.

> 1 part chamomile (money, gambling luck, hex-breaking, purification)
>
> 3 parts clove (luck, hex-breaking, sun, prosperity, protection, purification, dispelling negativity)
>
> 1 part patchouli (attraction, increasing the power of a spell, defense)
>
> 2 parts pine resin (assistance, balanced books, erasing business mistakes)

The recipe calls for resin because of the concentrated nature of the scent and magic in the resin. But if you can only find needles, increase the amount used. Chamomile is added for "gambling luck" because so much of business is a gamble. I am not advocating going to a casino with business funds. Because of chamomile's strong ties to gambling lore, consider making a strong infusion of chamomile flowers and rinsing your hands and the bottoms of your shoes before important meetings relating to the future of the business (loan meetings, meetings with corporate sponsors, potential partnerships, etc.).

Joyful Tidings

Holiday celebrations with family and friends.

> 2 parts cardamom (confidence, courage, creativity, passion, strengthens unions)
>
> 1 part marjoram (love, happiness, protection, family)
>
> 2 parts sandalwood (calm, centering, creativity, emotional stability, freedom, grounding)

Cardamom will give the smell of cinnamon without the potential lung irritation of the real thing. It will help bring everyone together to celebrate while enjoying each other's company. This incense is particularly beneficial if the celebrants are usually calculating how long is just long enough to stay to be polite before hitting the road or wondering how long before Aunt Judy says something terribly insulting. Burn thirty minutes before your guests arrive to "lay down the ground rules" early and allow the smoke to dissipate if it will cause any eye rolls.

Featured Herb: Sweetgrass

Hierochloe odorata.

United States. Fragrant grass shrub that grows to a height of 90 centimeters or 36 inches burned as an offering when imploring the spirits to bestow blessing. It has a soft, papery, vanilla fragrance reminiscent of straw or other sweet herbs.

Sweetgrass is a plant sacred to Native Americans and First Nations people. This member of the grass family is braided before it dries, so it dries and burns evenly. This plant is used to bring blessings in after banishing negativity from a space. Leaving a void after banishing would attract unwanted spirits, so plants like sweetgrass are employed to fill the space with beneficial energy instead. As with white sage, the popularity of this plant outside of indigenous communities has made it problematic to source for the communities for whom it is sacred. If this plant is essential to your practice, consider getting it directly from growers or harvesters within those communities.

Featured Resin: Piñon Pine

Pinus edulis.

United States. Native to the Southwest, this member of the pine family is a provider in the harshest of climes (edulis means "edible"). This tree's pine nuts are edible, the needles are steeped in water for tea, and the inner bark can be eaten as survival food as well. Pine nuts can be consumed raw, roasted, and even ground into flour for baked goods. Many local animals also rely on pine nuts for a ready food source in the unforgiving terrain of the Southwest.

Piñon pine, like many of the coniferous trees, has a clarifying, purifying, nurturing energy useful for cleansing work, connected with motherly energies and fertility. Bless a pinecone-shaped talisman in piñon resin smoke for fertility charms both physical and metaphorical. This is a resin of endurance and useful for any project or time when we need to be reminded that we are in control and we will persevere. It is friendship in adversity and can withstand many hardships. It is also useful for protection magic, so pine resin is a great ally for blessing a new home before moving in. If you are not able to lay your hands on the resin, get some pine needles (dried so you won't be cleaning up sap later) and scatter them over the floor. Let them lie there for twenty-four hours and then sweep them up. Afterward, burn the needles outside the home, cast them into a moving body of water, compost them, or dispose of them as you see fit. Burn pine inside the home as incense to reverse hexes. Beginning anew is the wheelhouse of the pine, so it can help erase business mistakes if you have learned your lesson. Piñon pine is centering, courageous, banishes evil, and helps us listen to our inner guides and find harmony with the situation at hand. In hex-breaking, it helps us find growth from the lesson in the hex, rather than just erasing it from our lives. All pine helps to bring awareness of our own life force and purify the aura.

9

Just Call the Whole Thing Off

When Not to Reach for the Sacred Smoke

This book has offered some incredible ideas for filling our lives with the gifts that nature has to offer, but every so often we have to consider our alternative options instead. What can we do and why should we?

Health Concerns?

As always, this book is not for diagnosing, treating, or preventing any illness; discuss health concerns with your healthcare professionals.

"Hey, I heard incense is terrible for you. I mean, it's smoke, right? Isn't smoking bad for you?"

Great question. First, anything done without moderation can be dangerous for you. Eight glasses of water a day should give us radiant skin, healthy organ function, and all sorts of benefits. Drink two gallons of water in an hour and your organs can shut down. If you are burning plants that you have an unknown allergy to or incense sticks of low quality or from a questionable source (I'm forever giving gas station incense the side eye), there can be issues.

The biggest problem is for people who already have a known health concern. If you have asthma, an upper respiratory infection, even seasonal allergies bothering you today that were not bothering you yesterday, take a beat and think about whether you really need this. If this is a spiritual need and not a want, perhaps there is another way to experience the ally you are seeking. If you'd like to explore frankincense, maybe you can make an anointing oil in a roller bottle rather than a smoke bath. If all you have is resin incense, look at using an oil burner and filling the reservoir with water and just one piece of resin instead. Once the water heats up, it can help the resin melt, and you will get the scent of the frankincense and its healing without aggravating your lungs. Each person has their own needs and health concerns, and no magic is worth risking your health and well-being.

The next point is that you aren't "smoking" the incense. None of these recipes are intended as smoking mixtures; they are burning, but not being directly inhaled as one would a cigarette. There is a much lower amount being inhaled and coming in contact with the lung tissue.

What to Use Instead

"My friend is coming over for ritual, and she has asthma. What can I use instead of incense to cleanse our ritual space?"

Thinking ahead makes you a great friend, as those with health concerns are usually the ones left feeling like the odd man out. By reaching out, you are making sure that your friend is engaged, involved, and appreciated. You can either use something traditional and premade like Florida Water or you can work together to create a batch of Florida Water as a part of the ritual (who doesn't love a crafty day with their best friend, where you get to take home a goodie bag!).

Florida Water (big batch recipe, great for gift giving)

1 liter 100-proof vodka or isopropyl alcohol from the pharmacy

1 dram lavender essential oil

1 dram orange essential oil

1 dram clove essential oil

Mix all the ingredients well. There are some other ingredients people love to add, like rose essential oil, but since I'm deathly allergic to rose, I don't have roses in my family version. If you are scaling down the recipe, start with equal amounts of the essential oils, and massage the mix until it smells right to you. After all, you are the one who is going to be using it.

For protecting your home, I also love to see people adding witch balls to their protection retinue. These beautiful decorative glass balls collect negative energy, and when the sun hits them, it blasts the power that has amassed and sends it back out into the universe where it can't harm anyone. Think of them as a passive protection system to add to the security of a home and really boost any other work that gets done around the house.

True Paranormal Events vs. Too Many Scary Movies

"OMG, what was that noise?! I bet it was a *demon*! Better grab the sage!"

No. Just no. Take a breath for me. It will be okay. Everything always seems really heightened in the dark. I know white sage is really popular right now, but it is really not the be-all and end-all. It definitely is not going to banish every nasty thing that people think it will. Nine times out of ten when people jump to conclusions and bust out the sage, their houses just need an energetic airing out, which is why the sage works. The same results could be accomplished just by opening the windows, so to speak. Sage is lovely for clearing energy, but so are *so* many other things. Pick any flower in this book, in fact—red geranium petals, lavender, red clover, a pinch of jasmine (not too much), clove (yes, they're a flower). The tenth time? It is something that is now grumpy at being disturbed from its comfy nest. (See chapter 4 for more on this). Demonic hauntings, possessions, etc., are truly rare, no matter what paranormal shows would have you believe. There are so many Ghost Investigator X and Scary Movie 24/7 channels now that we are inundated with reality television and scary movies, and it is hard to turn off our brain when it says, "It's okay to be scared sometimes." It allows us to deal with the things in our lives that really are scary in a healthy way.

And no matter what they say about how psychics and witches "aren't real," I know a few of the big-name groups, which use intuitives on every paranormal investigation they go on to tell them where to set up the cameras—even if they don't like to show them on camera or give them any credit.

When to Wait and See

"Little Tommy saw a ghost! Do I need to do a banishing?"

When I teach, I'm frequently asked about spirits, ghosts, and the like. "Little Johnny sees ghosts." Children are so much more open to these things because they haven't yet been told not to. My first question is always the same: I ask if it is bothering them, because there are a few different ways to go about handling that situation.

So just hold your horses. It is great that you are ready and willing to listen to your tiny human when they tell you what they have seen. Kids need to be heard. I love it when parents are ready and willing to take up their cauldrons in defense of their children especially. But just because they admitted to seeing a spirit does not tell us whether this spirit is harmful or benevolent (just because someone died doesn't make them a saint either!). Do your homework, and don't flip out either. Take a deep breath and allow your child to tell you more. You know your child better than I do. Is your child at the developmental age for an imaginary friend, or did they see a spirit? Many people report their parents writing off their first sighting of discarnate beings as an imaginary friend.

Sadly we can lose the ability to communicate with the other side when society tells us that we cannot see ghosts. Encourage dialogue with your child if it seems appropriate. If they seem frightened, then you can move forward with the materials outlined in chapter 4 and later in this chapter. Involve them in the process as much as you find appropriate to foster a sense of empowerment.

Casper the Friendly Ghost

There are a bunch of friendly ghosts out there. One of my first jobs after I graduated from high school and before I started college was as a live-in nanny for two little boys, Rick and Gunther. They were the sweetest little ones. Gunther was a toddler in diapers—walking, but not 100 percent on his feet yet. Rick was a bit older and headstrong already. It was my first week, and it was warm out. The windows were open, the sun was shining, and everyone was having a great morning. Breakfast was over, and we were playing. The TV was airing the boys' favorite show of the moment while we played trucks, and the boys were running around the love seat at top speed, giggling, when Gunther tripped. I dove to try and catch him because he had stripped off everything but his diaper (he's in college now and would be mortified at me telling you this), and I was terrified he'd hurt himself or at the least get rug burn. But I swear, Gunther floated gently to the floor. I thought my eyes were playing tricks on me as he giggled some more, got up, and went off again at top speed.

After lunch but before naptime the boys decided they both had to have the same remote control car at the same time and started fighting over it. It was naptime fighting—I got it. I placed the toy in time-out on top of the entertainment center and went up to put the boys down for a nap. When I came back downstairs, the toy car was driving itself around on top of the cabinet, back and forth. I checked the remote, and it was still on top of the entertainment center with its big red control button faceup.

I explained the things I saw throughout the day and later that night to the boys' mom after everyone else went to bed. As a witch, I wasn't worried about it myself, but if she was troubled, I'd offer my services since I lived there now too. "Oh, that's just Sarah," she said. It turns out that the large field behind the houses was empty because it was a historic battlefield. Sarah, she said, had been a nurse during the Revolutionary War, and another ghost she told me about in the home was named Jerome. She didn't need any help because these spirits were friendly and considered a part of the family.

Familial Spirits

"I think Uncle Craig is here to visit."

This is a double-edged sword. "Did you like Uncle Craig?" should always be the next question. If you want to keep your home open to familial spirits, it may end up being open season for any ghost. It is pretty tricky to put a "Craig only" filter on your door, and that is definitely not a beginner's topic.

If you want to banish all ghosts and keep the house ghost-free, Uncle Craig has got to go too. He can visit you outside the house. He can still hang out at Aunt Patti's; he just can't drop by your place for tea. Once you make the decision you want your house to be a "ghost-free zone," it is all or none until such a time as you undo your charms.

Keeping the Family Safe: Protection 101

An old traditional method of dispelling ghosts was to spit beans at the spirit of the departed, but I suppose I'd leave too if you were spitting beans at me. The tome never specified whether they were cooked or dried. Books from the Middle Ages through to the Victorian era suggested flashing ghosts your bits, and while that's laughable for some and scandalous for others (I'm firmly in the laughing camp!), their justification made me stop and think. Our sex characteristics, both primary (genitalia) and secondary (breasts), remind spirits of the departed of life and something they'll never have again: the vitality associated with sex.

If no one in your household is being bothered by the spirit, you can do something gentle and passive like work with ghostbusting salt.

If you have a child who is genuinely scared of a ghost or spirit and you want to seal the house against further intrusions from any spirits, bless the child with smoke from sandalwood (protection, love) and opoponax (astral strength) outside the home while Mom or loved ones sing happy, soothing songs to them. Try to remember how scary it is to be little. At the same time a separate team can

---

GHOSTBUSTING SALT

Mix a cup or two of salt (purification) depending on how big your house/apartment is with a tablespoon of dried garlic (banishing), a teaspoon of dried rosemary (banishing), and a teaspoon of dried nettle (protection). Grind this in a mortar and pestle if you have one. If you don't have one, just give it all a good stir with a wooden spoon. Let this mixture soak up the rays of the sun on a Sunday (protection), and then scatter it at night around the outside of the house on a Monday night (nurturing).

follow the instructions in chapter 4 for blessing the inside of the house. Once the child is sitting calmly with Mom, the inside of the home has been cleansed, and both teams have rejoined, take up some black salt and ring around the outside of the property counterclockwise (banishing). (In the case of an apartment, go around the whole building.)

BLACK SALT

2 cups kosher salt

½ cup iron filings (can be found in witchy shops or in science kits. This is also known as magnetic sand and is frequently sold with magnets.)

¼ cup black pepper

Optional:

¼ cup ashes from the fireplace

Lamp black

4 railroad spikes

Some hoodoo shops, botanicas, and even blacksmith supply shops sell railroad spikes, but if you live near railroad tracks and can *safely* scout along them, you can get lucky and find them for free. If you have friends or family members that work in electrical, ironwork, and other similar trades, they may be able to obtain them for you. If you find them, once the black salt is in place you can pound the spikes into the ground at the four corners of the property. Don't worry if the property lines are an odd shape; you can use the cardinal points of north, south, east, and west instead of the boundary to guide you. If you live in the concrete jungle where there's no hope of pounding steel into concrete without a jackhammer, no fear, just take the four spikes and place them in the four corners of the apartment, points out to defend the property from any ghostly visitors from now until you take up the spikes. For those of you worrying, "But salt melts in the rain," don't worry, the iron is the activating agent, the salt is to purify, and it all works in the end. And if you can find the railroad spikes but not the iron filings, just grab a metal file and put some elbow grease into it over the salt, or grab some steel wool (without the soap) and some scissors—after all, steel and iron are very closely related and magically their uses are linked.

When to Call the Professionals (and How to Find a Reputable One)

There are many different types of spirits, but we don't have the space here to spell out a whole paranormal dictionary. So let's look at some general rules.

Repeating energies of the Lady in Grey type that you see walking down grand staircases at the same time every day are just not an issue. They are not out to hurt anyone. They have no intelligence behind them. They are sort of like the wear spot on the carpet where you have walked over the same place over and over every day. It is just a feature of the house. It might feel a bit chilly there sometimes; it might not. There is no malice, no emotion at all usually, just someone going about their day in another time. This is nothing to call a professional for.

In chapter 4, I talked about the hierarchy of smoke allies and how each plant part has a different strength. These strengths resonate at different frequencies and can affect spirits, ghosts, and nasty entities differently. The more volatile oil something has, the higher its vibration and the heavier lifting it is able to do. If you have gone all the way through the hierarchy of plant allies and you still have a problem, it is time to call the professionals. It is great to want to fix your own issues, it is, but all the sage in the world is just going to cause more problems. There is no YouTube University for kicking out a poltergeist. You need someone with experience when you have malefic intent, scratches, noises, scared children, anxious pets, slamming doors, etc., and you have tried anything you dare to and failed.

The first time I saw a ghost throw something at me was in 2004. My group was called to a house where a teen girl, a baby, and the mother had all started waking up with scratches on them more expansive than a human hand could make. The mother reported feeling unsafe in the basement, so she started locking the basement door shut. "I told myself it was so that the baby couldn't fall down the steps, but really it was so the ghost couldn't come upstairs—isn't that silly?" When she went to grab the skeleton key off of the table to let us downstairs with our equipment to check it out, the key shot off the table, across the kitchen, and hit the wall, breaking the blue slab of agate on the key chain.

Google is great for a lot of things, but when it comes to ghostbusting, these reality TV shows have given a lot of people stars in their eyes—and electromagnetic field detectors. You are not looking for a paranormal investigation group; you are looking for magic workers. Some priests and pastors are good at banishing magic through prayer, but it is hard work and you have to know which books of the Bible are best for that kind of magic. (Yes, you can do magic with the Bible; there are lots of magic workers in the Bible Belt.)

The best thing you can do is ask people you trust to help you find a witch. Everyone knows one. If you start looking in the phone book for a psychic, chances are you are going to spot a con artist who is going to try to charge you ten thousand dollars for snake oil and do nothing. Should you expect to pay a professional for their time? Yes, everyone has a mortgage. Should *any* magical service cost you thousands of dollars, ever? No. No tarot reading, candle magic, hex-breaking, or anything should ever require that. Even if they tell you that the money isn't for them, that they are burning it to remove the curse, that's just another trick of con artists. Just say no, and move on to a witch instead.

If your friends don't know any witches personally, google your nearest New Age store and ask if they can recommend someone to cleanse a house of a spirit. Local shops always have their ear to the ground, although reputable shops are usually too busy running their own affairs to do the work themselves.

Afterword

This book is just a primer into the wide and wonderful world of working in concert with plants to cleanse, consecrate, protect, and bless your space. Every culture has its own unique and beautiful heritage in and history of incense, plants, and sacred smoke. Taking a single practice from one of them and trying to make it your own is not okay, but this book shares how you can experience the benefits of your own practice without appropriating any other culture's. It's about educating yourself and finding out about plants and resins that speak to you. Use the information here as a jumping-off point for your own explorations. Keep learning and growing. It's okay to make mistakes—just admit them, learn from them, and keep going. Do better.

INDEX OF RECIPES

BIBLIOGRAPHY

Blackthorn, Amy. *Blackthorn's Botanical Magic*. Newburyport, MA: Weiser Books, 2018.

Cunningham, Scott. *Cunningham's Encyclopedia of Magical Herbs*. 2nd ed., vol. I, 9th printing. Woodbury, MN: Llewellyn Publications, 2003.

Heath, Maya. *Magical Oils by Moonlight*. Franklin Lakes, NJ: New Page Books, 2004.

Holland, Eileen. *Holland's Grimoire of Magickal Correspondences: A Ritual Handbook*. Franklin Lakes, NJ: New Page Books, 2006.

Hyams, Gina, and Susie Cushner. *Incense: Rituals, Mystery, Lore*. San Francisco: Chronicle Books, 2004.

Kinkele, Thomas. *Incense and Incense Rituals: Healing Ceremonies for Spaces of Subtle Energy*. Twin Lakes, WI: Lotus, 2004.

Melody. *Love Is in the Earth: A Kaleidoscope of Crystals: The Reference Book Describing the Metaphysical Properties of the Mineral Kingdom*. Wheat Ridge, CO: Earth-Love, 1995.

Richardson-Read, Scott. "Saining Not Smudging—Purification and Lustration in Scottish Folk Magic Practice." Cailleach's Herbarium, February 10, 2019. Accessed February 28, 2019. *cailleachs-herbarium.com*.

Smith, Steven R. *Wylundt's Book of Incense.* York Beach, ME: Samuel
    Weiser, 1989.

"Sodium Selenite." Hazardous Substance Fact Sheet. Accessed
    November 15, 2018. *nj.gov.*

"Traditions of Northern Cyprus"
    Direct Traveller. Accessed November 3, 2018.
    www.directtraveller.com/guides/north-cyprus/traditions.

ABOUT THE AUTHOR

Amy Blackthorn has been described as an "arcane horticulturalist" for her life-long work with magical plants and teaching of hoodoo and plant-based magic. She incorporates her experiences in British Traditional Witchcraft with her horticulture studies. She is trained as a clinical aromatherapist and is ordained through the Gryphon's Grove School of Shamanism.

Amy has appeared on *HuffPost Live*, *Yahoo News*, and *Top 10 Secrets and Mysteries* (Episode: "Supernatural Abilities"). Her interviews have appeared in the *Associated Press*, the *Baltimore Sun*, *BankRate.com*, *Realtor.com*, the *Connecticut Post*, and more. She is the author of *Blacthorn's Botanical Magic: The Green Witch's Guide to Essential Oils for Spellcraft, Ritual & Healing* (Weiser, 2018).

Amy's company, Blackthorn Hoodoo Blends, creates tea based on old Hoodoo formulas. She lives in Delaware.

Visit her at *www.amyblackthorn.com*.